Rich Harvest

A Life in the Garden

DON HASTINGS

LONGSTREET
Atlanta, Georgia

Published by
LONGSTREET PRESS, INC.
A subsidiary of Cox Newspapers
A subsidiary of Cox Enterprises, Inc.
2140 Newmarket Parkway
Suite 122
Marietta, GA 30067

Printed in the United States of America

1st printing 1998

Library of Congress Catalog Card Number: 98-066363

ISBN: 1-56352-508-9

Jacket and book design by Jill Dible

To Betsy
and in loving memory of my mother and father,
Louise B. Hastings and Donald M. Hastings

Prologue

When my friends at Longstreet Press asked me to write a book about my gardening experiences, I balked at the idea. It seemed too high a mountain for me to climb. But I had three determined enthusiasts — Betsy, my wonderful wife; Chris, my son and coauthor of *Month-by-Month Gardening in the South*; and John Yow, my good friend and fantastic editor at Longstreet.

Still, how on earth could I ever put into words sixty-plus years of working with plants, and, more importantly, would my memories help others grow plants better? Then I remembered something I wrote in the introduction to my first gardening book: "Gardening is not a study; it's an experience." The more I thought about this phrase, the deeper I felt the truth in it.

Our society seems to live by instruction manuals: attach "A" to "B" or double-click on this or that icon. But I found in writing my first books that there can be no precise manual for gardening in the South — or anywhere else. I could give the basic information, but I could not supply the will, desire, and love of plants necessary for successful gardening. With the help of my own experiences and those of others, I learned how to grow plants, but I was able to grow plants well only after they became a rich part of my life.

So, accepting Longstreet's challenge, I have written a book about the experiences I've had over many years of dealing with plants here in the Southern United States, as well as in strange and wonderful places like the Sahara Desert in Egypt, an island in the Philippines, and a former jungle in Malaysia. Some of my experiences may seem exotic because of their far-flung locales, but they are not much different from your experiences wherever you have grown plants.

Many of you have come south from other places with very different climates and soil conditions; others have left the South and found an unfamiliar gardening environment. In either case, you may have wanted to grow the same plants in your new locale that you loved in your old.

My grandmother Hastings was from Ohio, where she had easily grown lilacs and peonies. My grandfather and their sons, including my father, insisted that these plants would not do well in the South, probably would not survive. But she wanted her favorites, and she grew them — with great success. Nelson Crist, one of my mentors at the family company, planted Red Horse chestnut and laburnum, which nobody believed would grow, but they did because he wanted them to.

I have known highly trained "experts" who were very poor plantsmen. On the other hand, some of the best specimen plants I have ever seen have been in country yards or on country porches, grown by housewives who simply wanted them, then nurtured them until they were a beautiful part of the family.

There's no magic to gardening. Success comes from the heart, from the love of plants. Each experience is an expression of that love. Some things you can learn from books: when to plant, how deep to plant, when to prune, when and how to fertilize, even which plants might grow best for you. But reading the manuals is not going to make your plants grow well.

Your feeling for the plants you want to grow — how you love, nurture, and care for them — is the most important thing: the most rewarding for you, and most crucial for your plant's utmost well-being. Because of unpleasant childhood experiences with them, I have no desire to plant junipers, so I don't. But I love camellias. Guess what? They do fabulously for me.

Contents

Rich Harvest

Epigraph

The landscape planting is a picture; it must have a canvas. This canvas is the greensward. Upon this, the artist paints with tree and bush and flower, the same as the painter does upon his canvas with brush and pigments. The opportunity for artistic composition and structure is nowhere so great as in the landscape garden, because no art has such a limitless field for the expression of its emotions. There can be no rules for landscape gardening, any more than there can be for painting. The operator may be taught how to hold the brush or plant the tree, but he remains the operator; the art is intellectual and emotional and will not confine itself in precepts.

— L. H. Bailey

Part One

The Garden Forever

*And the Lord God planted a garden toward the east,
in Eden; and there He placed the man whom He had
formed.*

*And out of the ground the Lord God caused to grow
every tree that is pleasing to the sight and good for
food; the tree of life also in the midst of the garden,
and the tree of the knowledge of good and evil.*

— Genesis 2:8–9
NASB

Gardens have been essential to our existence since the earliest times. The ancient Persians and Greeks developed garden areas around their homes, which the Greeks called *paradeisos*. From their word for *garden* comes our word for *paradise*. To the ancients and to us moderns, paradise connotes beauty, happiness, and peace. In other words — at least to my mind — the garden.

But there's one other quality essential to the garden, I believe. Way back during my student days, I saw a garden with a stunning three-quarter nude female carved from exquisite marble placed as though she were stepping into a pool. It was a shock to us young horticulturists, especially when the gardener appeared and we realized that she was the model for the statue! Fortunately, both were beautiful.

Thinking about that garden over the years has helped me refine my definition of what a garden is — or at least what I think it ought to be. Because what I concluded was that that statue was entirely appropriate; it was that lady's garden, in her own private place, and she was stamping her own personality on it. I like that, and it made me realize that, in addition to being havens of beauty and happiness, gardens ought to be expressions of an individual personality.

Today gardens are everywhere — large estate gardens, botanical gardens, and public parks with garden areas. But the gardens I love are private gardens, where individuals find their own paradise while planning, planting, nurturing, and enjoying plants.

This kind of garden might be a small plot in the back of a home, or an elaborate undertaking nestled in the landscape. It can even be a group of houseplants, a hanging basket on the porch, or a burn plant, *aloe vera*, in the kitchen. Gardens can also be in the mind, as dreams for the future or memories of the past. What brings a garden to life is the gardener who expresses his dreams in a plan and then his personality in its execution.

Please don't confuse a garden with "the landscape." To me, the landscape is the overall picture, including public areas, whereas the garden is confined and private. Flower beds and vegetable gardens in front of homes may add beauty and function to a piece of property, but they sometimes make me feel like I am looking into the owner's living room. I believe a garden should be a place of quiet repose, not an advertisement.

Don't get me wrong. I love beautifully landscaped homes, with flowers and shrubs appealingly placed as an invitation to the outsider, like draperies in a window or ornate entranceways. But such ornaments, however beautiful, do not take the place of a garden, which is a separate place, a personal and private paradise.

Many years ago I wanted to do something about the area in back of our house. I didn't know just what to do, but I had never liked the way it was planted. Over a period of about two years, I struggled with this problem, putting idea after idea on paper and then tearing the pages up. Edith Henderson, the wonderful landscape architect, came by one Sunday, so I asked for her help. She quickly sketched out a few plans, and it was like turning on a light in a dark room. I just had never thought of developing the back the way she suggested. She didn't tell me what plants to plant or even where to place flower beds, but she gave me the structure within which I could have plants we love.

I think of Edith when people ask me, as they often do, why they need a plan for their garden or landscape. Think of the plan as an outline, the canvas on which you paint the picture, filling in the lines with the trees, shrubs, vines, or flowers that you like and want in your garden. The point is, again, that your garden should be an expression of you. The "plan" becomes a problem when it imposes the values of the architect or designer on your landscape. Edith's plan, of course, helped me develop my backyard area in a way that expressed my personality and my desires, not hers.

In the South of my younger days, when people in the country referred to "the garden," they meant a place to grow vegetables. Whether in Extension Service bulletins, rural newspapers, or common conversation, talk of "the garden" never included flowers, shrubs, trees, or fruits. Many years later, I supervised a vegetable testing project on a small island in the center of the Philippine archipelago. To my surprise, people there defined a garden as a place to grow vegetables, not flowers or fruits. Our 150-acre testing ground became known as "Mr. Don's garden," and it made me feel pleasurably at home when each morning the crew would ask what I wanted them to do in my garden.

We are now more inclined to define a garden as a place to grow flowers and nothing else. My feeling is that gardens are places for plants, any kind of plants except maybe weeds (even though there are some modernists who think gardens should be natural and include weeds as well). There is no rule governing what kinds of plants a garden must contain. Because of space limitations, we might grow herbs in one bed, tomatoes in another, beans on an arbor, fruits as flowering trees, and flowers for cutting. The only rule, as far as I'm concerned, is that your garden afford pleasure to you, your family, and your friends.

Though personal gardens are my favorites, I enjoy visiting estate gardens, botanical gardens, plant collections, and well-kept parks. These gardens not only introduce us to plants we might like to grow ourselves; they also allow us to view plants at full maturity, which, of course, retail nurseries cannot do. I remember the first time I saw a relatively mature dawn redwood growing at Auburn

University. It was beautiful and it was huge, and it made me realize that the small plants people were setting out like crazy would soon be so crowded they would be unsightly. Well-maintained estate and botanical gardens have the great advantage of letting us see the more-or-less finished product.

Another thing I love about estate and botanical gardens is that they are seldom influenced by fads. Landscape architects and designers, nurserymen, and gardeners are often led like sheep by the hype for a new plant. I left Atlanta in the early eighties when people still planted dogwoods, one of our finest trees. When I returned, my city had gone nuts over Bradford pears. They were everywhere. They lined the streets and were massed around commercial buildings, in front yards, backyards, and anywhere else a tree would grow. But what did anyone really know about these plants?

I had planted one myself shortly after they were introduced (before the craze had become epidemic). We were overseas when this plant began to grow rapidly, so I failed to prevent the development of the narrow crotches to which they are extremely prone. One day a windstorm toppled half the tree, bringing down the power line and messing up the yard but, fortunately, sparing the house. A few years later, Hurricane Opal showed the world what high winds can do to these trees. Opal's path was littered with broken Bradford pears and structure damage caused by their limbs and trunks crashing down.

The proliferation of these trees reminded me of a time when I was just out of college, and a friend and I went on a fishing trip to North Central Canada. We were on the long desolate road from Nipigon to Kirkland Lake and North Bay when we realized that ninety percent of the homes had blue roofs. Since both of us were interested in marketing, we decided that the blue roof salesman in this area must have been one of the top roof salesmen in Canada. Maybe there was a better reason for all the blue roofs in that part of Canada, but it seemed to us that people had blue roofs either because of a great sales job or because everybody else had one. I felt the same way when I returned to North Georgia and found Bradford pears everywhere I looked. In a similar vein, I was in Ireland not long ago and noticed that every new home seemed to have a Kwanzan cherry. The blue roof salesman must have also reached that pristine country.

Fortunately, many gardeners resist fads; they are attracted to plants with individuality and unique qualities, rather than those that are suddenly popular. Old estates, botanical gardens, and collections are filled with all sorts of plants that will help your landscape and garden reflect your own personality. Be a keen observer before you buy a new-rage plant or a blue roof from a super salesman.

Another way to make your garden personal is to use plants in different ways. One of my friends wanted a pyracantha to espalier on a wall. I went through my "It's tough to keep a pyracantha looking nice" lecture, but he nodded and said, "I have always wanted one." He loved that pyracantha against its gray wooden background and made it into one of the most beautiful espaliers I have ever seen. He learned how to prune it properly to keep its form while leaving shoots that would bloom and set berries.

Of course, there are limits. I am old enough to remember the days when people made images of animals and other objects out of hedges. Yards had sheep, rabbits, urns, and all sorts of other things shaped out of hedge plants, usually privet, which is a mess at best. I have seen gardens in Europe filled with interestingly shaped plants, but they were not in the front yard for all to see as they drove by. Espaliers, topiaries, and other shaped plants can make a garden unique and beautiful, and they are a wonderful way to imprint your personal touch. But I would caution you not to overdo shaping plants, or your personality might be imprinted too intensely.

Many fine gardens are developed around plants of special interest. Rose gardens, cutting gardens, perennial gardens, vegetable gardens, and herb gardens are some typical examples. There is a special challenge in becoming an expert in a single type of plant.

Many years ago I was on a train from Victoria Station in London to a nearby suburb. The rail line went through an area of identical attached houses, each with a small open area between the back of the house and the rail line, and the great majority of these small backyards contained a garden. Some were for roses, some for dahlias, some for perennials, and a few for only vegetables. I saw none with only grass and rarely one with junk. Each garden reflected a special interest of the person tending it. I enjoyed the ride very much and delighted in seeing how these urban blue-collar workers preserved and displayed their individuality even while being jammed so close to their neighbors. They probably never realized how much pleasure they gave to the enormous numbers of people who had fleeting looks at their gardens, which they had developed solely for themselves and their families.

Once, I had the rare opportunity of going to the Chelsea Flower Show in London. Chelsea is probably the premier flower show in the world, attracting hundreds of exhibitors and hundreds of thousands of people. Among the rich and famous there were many who probably had developed tiny garden plots by rail lines. Fine clothes and jewels held no status as we looked at a beautiful new clematis, spectacular roses, arbored laburnums, and massive displays of orchids. Each of us had a dream of how we might grow such plants back home in our own garden. On that day at the Chelsea show, we were simply lovers of plants who had come to see the finest garden exhibition in the world.

A love of plants, along with a deep curiosity about them, is the driving force behind a garden. First you see a plant or read about it. You want one, so you search until you find it; then you learn how to plant and care for it. As it grows bigger and better with your love and care, it becomes a part of your gardening experience and an important part of your life. I have tremendous curiosity about plants, especially what place they are native to, who discovered them, and how they got here. I suppose the history of a plant has little relevance to how it will look and perform in my garden, but it makes a plant much more personal when I know what some hardy soul went through to bring it here.

Not all plant explorers were savory characters. The purpose of the voyage headed by the infamous Captain Bligh of the *HMS Bounty* was to collect breadfruit plants in Polynesia for planting in the British colonies in the Caribbean. Many others with more palatable personalities and reputations endured extreme hardships — sometimes even death — to bring home interesting plants from far-off places.

I don't like to eat okra, but when I discovered how it was brought from its homeland in India to Egypt, where it found favor with the Pharaohs, I became fascinated with it — at least as a plant if not as a vegetable. Imagine carefully packing the seed of any plant, much less okra, on camels for a trip covering many months and thousands of miles. That is the way okra moved westward from its home in India.

Gardens tell much about the people of a country and their culture. One of my favorite pastimes during a business trip is to visit the parks and search out the small gardens. I try to identify trees and shrubs selected by the city fathers, perhaps centuries ago, or see what types of colorful plants people of a city enjoy. Well-planted cities like Seattle, Portland, London, Paris, Copenhagen, Helsinki, Hong Kong, and Singapore show the value the people of those cities place on making urban areas beautiful. Unfortunately, today's politicians seldom give high priority to beautifying the cityscape because trees don't vote and people do, so money is spent on "basic needs" of voters while environmental beauty is neglected.

Ultimately though, private plantings determine

whether or not a place preserves and enhances its natural beauty. Charleston, South Carolina, for example, has a few worthy parks, but the beauty of the city lies in the homes and businesses that plant even the smallest spots. As you stroll down Meeting Street, Bull Street, Bay Street, or many other small ones, a peek over a wall or a stop at a gate is likely to reveal an enchanting garden.

Finally, it pays to remember that not all gardens are created by man. God's garden — that part of our planet that remains unspoiled — cannot be overlooked when we think of paradise on earth. My own world, the Southern United States, has extraordinary natural areas that are truly unique. Few places are as awesome as the Okeefenokee Swamp, or as beautiful as the Southern Appalachian Mountains where cold streams play beside banks covered with mountain laurel and rhododendron. Above the shrubs but under the canopy of white pine and hemlock, magnificent *Stewartia ovata* drop their beautiful flowers on the forest floor. In parts of these mountain gardens, as in coastal-plain swamps, man is more rare than a white tail deer or a swamp alligator lying motionless after a meal.

I have been in many parts of the world where man's intrusion into God's garden has not destroyed natural beauty. I have been fortunate enough to appreciate the splendor to be found in a few palms and a bit of grass around a desert oasis, a shoreline of a tropical island, and the dense undergrowth of a tropical rain forest — all parts of the paradise created by God.

In the end, gardening is our way of using plants to recreate what God gave us to begin with — a private, personal, peaceful, and quiet place that's as close as we can get to paradise on earth.

Chapter One

"As a Tree Is Bent"

'Tis education forms the common mind;
Just as the twig is bent, the tree is inclined.
—Alexander Pope

"As a tree is bent, so will it grow," my mother frequently admonished me when I was little. She referred to plants when making almost any kind of important point, often altering time-honored sayings to better fit a situation — like lecturing me. My grandfather, father, and mother were all horticulturists and lived in a world of plants. From day one, which I don't happen to remember, I have too.

The place where I grew up, near rural Lovejoy, Georgia, was H.G. Hastings Co.'s 1,500-acre seed farm and nursery supervised by my father, Donald M.

Hastings. My father was the youngest son of Harry G. Hastings, an eminent Southern horticulturist and seedsman who had founded the company in 1889. My mother, Louise Hastings, was a respected horticulturist in her own right, and frankly the best gardener of us all. It was she who planned the spacious terraced gardens which lay to the north of the house and which evolved over the years into an ever-more-beautiful place for family and friends to enjoy.

It was a measure of this special environment that even when things wouldn't grow, they did anyway. The field in front of the house had once been used to grow narcissus bulbs but the venture had not been profitable. In fact, one section of the field was never again used for crop production because it was a low and soggy place where tractors got stuck in less than perfect conditions. Here the neglected narcissus bulbs multiplied like mad, producing a field full of such beautiful blooms each spring that people would stop along the highway just to gaze at the splendor.

As a youngster, my only connection to my mother's gardens was my propensity for falling into one of the decorative fish pools and having to be extracted by our gardener Willie Pine. Otherwise I stayed clear, much preferring to climb the big sweet gum tree in the backyard or even to play hide and seek with my sister in the hedges. However, when I was twelve, the garden took on an ominous reality.

"I want you to start helping Willie in the garden," Momma said in her "don't argue with me" tone. Summer in Georgia is hot, especially hot in that garden where tall hedges kept out any hint of a breeze. Black gnats swarmed everywhere, and I hated every minute of it. I made the mistake of telling Momma that the garden was a hot, miserable, and useless place.

"Besides," I said, "I hate messing in the dirt."

She swatted me hard on the shoulder, then lectured forever, it seemed, on the beauty of the soil, its fresh smell, its life-giving properties. "Don't ever let me hear you call soil *dirt*. Soil is wonderful, dirt is not." She convinced me, and I'm still convinced. Every time I hear that gardening ad about playing in the dirt, I remember that swat and Momma's admonition. In her heavenly garden, I know she hates hearing that jingle even more than I do.

The next summer I escaped by working in the company's nursery, and I believe that's where my tree began to bend. The farm was separated into two divisions: field crops and nursery stock. The field part specialized in producing seeds of Hastings Prolific Corn, Hastings Hundred Bushel Oats, Clemson Spineless Okra, Stone Mountain Watermelon, and cotton. The nursery produced 150,000 roses per year, several thousand Chinese chestnut trees, hundreds of *Magnolia grandiflora* seedlings, and large numbers of other trees and shrubs.

We started work at sunup and stopped at sundown, with an hour and a half for lunch, which is a long, long day for a scrawny thirteen-year-old boy. We hoed a lot. Mr. Watts, who headed the nursery, would say, "You boys sharpen your hoes and go cut the weeds in the cannas." Since Mr. Watts refused to have the modern "gooseneck" hoe in the nursery, ours were always the old "ringneck" kind, made to chop cotton and heavy as lead. We had files to keep our hoe blades sharp, but it was still hard work, especially when Mr. Watts sent us to hoe nut grass out of the canna field. We rested by leaning on the hoe handle, which always brought a stern reprimand: "You boys are going to bend those hoe handles if you don't quit leaning on them." When Mr. Watts didn't laugh after scolding us, we knew he was serious, so we would chop like crazy until he was out of sight.

I didn't like hoeing then and still don't like it today, but working in the fields was heaven compared to working in Momma's hot garden. For one thing, I worked with boys my own age who became my first best friends. One of them, Glenn Dorsey, my good friend to this day and one of Georgia's best nurserymen, still has a garden center and nursery adjacent to the fields where we worked. And for another thing, I was beginning to enjoy learning how to make plants grow.

~

Roses

If hoeing nut grass in the cannas was a start, my education continued apace when we began to work in the rose fields. We learned how to doodle roses; then a month later we learned the artful techniques of cutting bud wood from last year's plants and bud-grafting on this year's understock. My mentors were A. D. "Coot" Morris and Wilbert Grissom, the best-hearted and most wonderful coworkers anyone could have.

Coot never talked about his background except to say that he grew up near Hazelhurst in South Georgia and that his ancestors had come from somewhere in Europe. He called Momma "Ma Hastings," something no one else — not even my sister or I — would ever think of doing. Wilbert was born on the company's farm when it was near Hoganville, before my grandfather moved the farming operations to Lovejoy. Wilbert was the son of Emma Grissom, a wonderful person who served the farm community in many ways but was most noted for having delivered, in her own estimate, "more than five hundred white and black babies" during her lifetime. Emma would tell us in a dispassionate way how her grandmother had been enticed onto a slave ship by being invited to a huge feast when times were so bad in Africa that the people of her village were starving. Wilbert's extended family also produced the famous baseball player, Marquis Grissom, who looks a lot like Wilbert did. Whenever I see Marquis play, I think of Wilbert tutoring me under the hot summer sun a long time ago.

One hundred thousand or more blooming roses in a single field was a sight to behold, but until I went to work in the nursery, I had no idea of the expertise necessary to produce the many varieties we grew. Momma loved roses and used them in arrangements for which she was noted, but Dad wouldn't let her into the fields to cut their blossoms. Her idea of how to make the cut was based on her vision of the arrangement and not on what was best for an individual plant, so he always cut what she needed. On countless Sunday mornings, as I followed along with a bucket of water for him to stick the cut flowers in, Dad explained the wonderful science of rose propagation. But it went in one ear and out the other; I paid no attention to the process until I became a part of it.

Rose propagation started in December when the full-time nursery crew removed the tops of the wild multiflora roses on which the bud had been grafted the previous summer. As a result of this pruning, the single bud the budders had inserted on the stem would be forced out come springtime. To earn some extra Christmas money, the farm women would take these huge piles of prunings and make cuttings about eight inches long, which they then bundled and wrapped in damp burlap cut from old seed bags. The damp bundles were buried in a huge bin of sand erected near the bell tower in the commissary yard, where they stayed until a spell of good weather in January or early February. Then the cuttings could be stuck directly in the field as the new understock. By June when I started work after school was out, these cuttings had grown rapidly into large plants that were ready to bud.

We called it budding, but it is really bud-grafting, a precise and exacting process. Mr. Watts was the perfect manager for such an operation, since he insisted that everything be done in order and just right.

The first step was doodling, a chore that reminded me a lot of working in Momma's garden. We dreaded the day when Mr. Watts would say, "Boys, it's time to doodle the roses." When rose stock is prepared for budding, soil is plowed against the stems to soften the part where the bud-graft will be made. About a month after this "throwing to," the understock is ready to doodle. The men hoed between the plants with a short-handled, specially-forged doodling implement while we younger boys crawled down the row on our hands and knees, carefully raking the loose soil away from the stems. By the time we reached the end of a row, we were covered with soil (not dirt). After doodling several long rows, Mr. Watts would let us take a break. We flopped down on the loose soil and rested, not conscious of the hot July sun beating down or the black gnats buzzing around our eyes and noses. The most important lesson I learned while doodling was how to doze off in extremely uncomfortable situations, something I can still do.

The next step was getting the bud wood ready for the budders in the field. Mr. Watts went to the field of roses budded the previous summer, which were now growing profusely. He cut shoots which had the buds we would use, bringing them back in meticulously labeled buckets. We would sit in the shade and carefully remove all the thorns from each cutting. Handling the thorny shoots was a real pain, but I liked any job when we sat in the shade.

Before Mr. Watts let us boys try to bud or tie, we "laid boards." The understock we grafted on was big and bushy by the time it was ready to bud, and it was hard to reach under the foliage to make the cut and slip in the bud. So Mr. Watts had special budding boards made out of 1 x 6 x "tough for me to handle" lengths with 2 x 4 chocks underneath. In our crew, Coot budded while sitting on the board, Wilbert tied while kneeling facing the board, and I laid the boards. I would carefully lay a board upside down with the chocks up in the row right next to the stock plants, then turn the board over with the chocks down onto the tops of the stock, which bent them over and exposed their bare stems. I had to straighten and clean the soil off each stem so as not to dull Coot's budding knife. If I left a stem with grit on it, Coot would make me reclean all I had prepared, so I tried to do it right the first time. In addition to the budder, the tyer, and the board-layer, each crew had three of these long boards, plus a funny pushcart with a canopy, which Mr. Watts had invented to keep the hot sun from scorching the exposed buds until the board was removed and the multiflora tops sprang up, shading the stem.

Budding is a combination of speed, accuracy, and skill, and you need a sharp knife to make a clean cut. Coot would make a vertical cut straight up the stem, then a horizontal cut at the top to make a "T." Then he would open the "T" with the budding quill without tearing the tender bark, and insert the bud without touching it with his fingers. Then Wilbert would tie the bud in place with a rubber strip. Mr. Watts scolded us when he saw us handle a bud with our fingers, since the salt in our sweat could damage the tender tissue.

As soon as Coot and Wilbert started down the last board, I would quickly lay two boards ahead, straighten and clean the stock, then lie down in the row for a quick nap — which I had to time perfectly. If Coot and Wilbert were about to run out of prepared stock, one of them would nail me with a clod of dirt (not soil).

Of course, learning to bud and tie roses was my goal. Wilbert taught me how to tie and Coot taught me the art of budding. I never became as good as they were, but I was fairly good. They could bud and tie over two thousand a day while my best day was twelve hundred. More importantly, they always had a live bud count of 75 percent or higher while I did well to reach 60 percent.

~

Other Lessons

My experiences working those summers when I was young shaped many of the opinions and attitudes that are still with me. Take my dislike of juniper, for example. When we weren't working in the rose fields, we boys had all sorts of jobs, like picking bagworms off junipers. Mr. Watts would send us off to the field with buckets, into which we dropped the bagworms after we tugged and pulled the hideous things off the evergreen shrubs. This was always a Saturday morning job since we had our minds on getting the afternoon off, which made us less than effective at almost anything else. When the big bell rang for "quitting time," we would hurry to the commissary where we always assembled. Mr. Watts had us dump the buckets of bagworms into a big pile on the ground. He poured kerosene over the pile, then "stuck a match" to it, resulting in an inferno of miserable slithering larvae coming out of their cocoons. "Better than arsenic," he would say, then laugh.

We boys decided there must be a better way to get rid of bagworms, so we spread the word that they made fine fishing worms, hoping beyond hope that the workers would send their wives and children to pick them off for bait. Guess what? Nobody fell for it.

My aversion to okra also goes back to those days. One of our jobs was to cut their dried pods for seeds in August when the weather was hot and humid and the gnats were at their peak. I can still feel the okra spines under my collar and the horrible itching they caused. We would tie a bandanna tightly around our buttoned collars and strings around the ends of our shirtsleeves, but the okra spines would still get in. Never have I known such discomfort.

Much later in my life our Malaysian project grew hundreds of acres of okra, including 'Clemson Spineless,' which my father had introduced decades before. Okra in

Malaysia also presented harvesting difficulties, even though it was cut fresh instead of being left to dry on the plant for seed. One morning during harvest, a huge commotion in the okra field brought all the field supervisors running. An Indian woman with her harvest bucket almost full reached to cut a pod and found herself face to face with a fifteen-foot flared-out king cobra. She screamed and threw the bucket up in the air, probably scaring the cobra as badly as it had scared her. At any rate, she survived the incident, but my memories of okra-induced itching paled in comparison.

On the other side of the coin, my love for the smell of fresh-cut grain comes directly from when we "combined" the fields during those summers of my youth. In earlier days at the farm, they had used a "binder," which cut the ripe grain stalks and bundled them together in shocks. The shocks were stacked and left in the field to dry, then taken to the barn area and run through a thrasher to remove the kernels. In my time, however, we harvested most of our wheat and oats with a "combine," a machine which both cuts the grain stalks and removes the seed while still in the field.

Mr. Dorsey, Glenn's father, was the field crops manager and in charge of grain production. He let us boys ride the combine and push the tied sacks of grain down the chute onto the ground, where a truck would come along to pick them up. We watched with excitement as the combine went round and round and the circle of uncut grain grew smaller and smaller. All sorts of things lived in a grain field, including field birds, mice, and best of all, rabbits. All these creatures retreated inward, trying to escape the increasing noise of the combine, until there was no place to go. Meanwhile, we stood ready to jump off the platform and chase whatever came out.

The mice emerged first, which alerted us for rabbits — the real prize. When a rabbit — or maybe several — came scampering out and raced across the field, the whole operation stopped. Tractor drivers, truck drivers, loaders, and we boys would choose our quarry and enter the chase. Wilbert, who despite his large size had those wonderful Grissom genes, would outrace young and old, then dive to the ground and capture the rabbit for his wife Arabelle to prepare a feast with that night.

There were other times, usually because of weather, when we had to cut some of the grain the old-fashioned way — with the binder. One Saturday when I was four-teen, Mr. Watts sent us boys with the field crew to toss the shocks of grain onto the truck and then take them to the thrasher.

We boys were walking along the row of shocks, pitch-forking them up onto the truck as it rolled by, for Wilbert and Bennie to stack them properly. I picked up a shock and tossed it up, then turned to get the next shock and was staring at a coiled copperhead. Wilbert saw the snake and yelled, "Hit him with the pitchfork!" Too scared to have any sense, I started stabbing at the snake, just making it madder and madder.

"Hit him with the *side* of the pitchfork," Wilbert yelled. I wound up and hit the snake as hard as I could with the side of the pitchfork, killing it dead as a doornail. But when I came down on the snake, I broke the handle of the pitchfork "slap in two," as Wilbert and Bennie told everybody at the thrasher.

That night I felt funny, and by the next day I was really getting sick. By Monday my left hand had swelled up about three times its size, and by Tuesday the telltale streaks of blood poisoning could be seen on my wrist. Momma rushed me to the hospital in Atlanta, where the doctor opened up my hand and found a huge pocket of infection eating away inside. Heavy callouses had built up in my palm next to my fingers, and somehow a rose thorn had gotten stuck underneath a callous, starting the infection that burst loose when I hit the snake with my pitchfork.

It took a while for me to be able to work again, and in the meantime I got to go to Florida with Dad to inspect the watermelon crop. Unfortunately, my hand healed in time for the okra harvest in late August.

Working on the farm was the hardest work I have ever

done, but probably the most rewarding. It bent my tree in the direction of horticulture, and I grew that way. But besides the art and technique of growing things, I learned about people and about life. I made $2.15 a day for 14-plus hours of hard work, and was happy and proud for being able to earn it. I learned not to be jealous of those who made more, nor feel superior to those who made less.

I also learned to be tolerant — at least somewhat — of what I thought was ignorance. One of the longest and worst arguments I have ever heard was between our blacksmith and one of the German war prisoners assigned to the farm during World War II. It continued off and on for several days.

Almost all of our workers, including me, went home for lunch, where we would take an hour and a half off during the midday heat. After lunch we went back to the commissary and shop area to wait for Mr. Wooten, the superintendent, to ring the big bell sending us back to work. I liked to go back a little early so I could stand around and listen to what was going on on the farm. One day I noticed a group of workers gathered around the blacksmith and the German, who were having an argument that was turning into a shouting match. I wedged myself between Coot and Wilbert and asked what was going on. They explained that the blacksmith and the German were fussing about whether the sun moved around the earth or the earth moved around the sun.

Back then workers talked a lot about the sun in its relationship to time. A few years before I went to work, the government had moved all of Georgia out of the Central time zone into the Eastern. (Before the change, the dividing line split Georgia in two.) This changed the time the sun came up and set, according to the clock. Georgia farmers had grown up with the sun coming up at a certain time on the clock and thought the government was being used by the devil to mess up their lives. As a result, the old-timers kept their watches set on the old Central time, which they called sun time, while those who didn't care set theirs on Eastern time, which they called government time. When the government instituted daylight saving time on top of this, it threw everything into chaos. Many who had accepted Eastern time now refused to be prodded any further by a government under the control of who knew what. Mr. Wooten, for instance, rang the bell on regular government time, but refused to use new government time. If you asked any reasonable person like Mr. Watts, Coot, or Wilbert what time it was, they would ask, "Sun time, regular time, or new time?"

I listened intently to the argument. The blacksmith believed the sun moved through the sky and quoted Bible verses to prove his point, while the German indignantly held the scientific view that the earth turned, making it seem like the sun moved. It was my first introduction to conflict between religion and science, and neither man was about to give an inch. Wilbert and Coot just laughed, but I couldn't stand it. As a young plant scientist, I was just dying to enter the fray — and certain that I could make reason prevail. But my mentors convinced me to bite my tongue, and they were right. I learned that day that there is no use arguing with people about what they believe. We all had to work together, whether it was sun time or government time, and whether it was the earth or the sun that did the rotating.

In addition to Wilbert and Coot, some of my non-gardening lessons came from my father, who was not only a respected horticulturist but a good man. On weekends, when I was not off riding my horse around the farm, I would sometimes go with Dad to his trial grounds and watch him "note the trials." This wasn't as exciting as riding six miles across country to Fayetteville, but it did continue my education.

Dad felt a deep sense of responsibility for the seed we listed for sale in the catalog. Many of our vegetable seeds were supplied by contract growers who had fine reputations, but Dad still wanted to be sure they were keeping our seed lines pure, so every year he tested each kind. The trial grounds were a beautiful sight, like our rose fields, with big shiny stakes at the beginning of each variety and long, straight rows of plantings in flat, fertile ground.

Dad also tried all the new varieties that claimed to be much better than the old favorites. For easy comparison, he had the new ones planted right next to the ones we listed. Some members of the firm weren't crazy about these comparisons because they were hot to profit on whatever the newest rage was in the vegetable seed world. Momma said, "Your father is as stubborn as a mule. He's got to make sure the new ones are really better." And he did make sure, or he refused to list them in the catalog. Over the years I took a cue from him in my huge overseas vegetable projects, and always set up trials to test new varieties before we planted two or three hundred acres of something that could conceivably flop.

Frankly, as a young teenager I wasn't always happy sitting in the hot sun watching Dad take meticulous notes. I had enough of the hot sun during the week. I would much rather have been riding Lady with the wind in my face. But I couldn't help being impressed when he showed me the results. "Hey," he would say, "look at the difference between this *new* crookneck squash and our regular Yellow Summer Crookneck." Sure enough, the old standard from our catalog was a lot better than the new "bigger and four times better" variety being touted by some seedsman.

Dad believed that our customers deserved honesty and integrity from us, and I developed a deep respect for his business ethic.

~

Higher Ed

By the time I finished high school, I was a practicing horticulturist and could even enjoy a walk through Momma's garden without suffering any ill effect. I was glad I had escaped working in it, grateful for my time in the fields, and happy to begin my formal horticultural training at Cornell University in Ithaca, New York.

Cornell University was a phenomenal place to study right after World War II. L. H. Bailey, the father of agricultural and horticultural science, was still alive, occasionally sharing his life and perspectives with us. The giants of American agricultural and horticultural science, John Cornman, George H. M. Lawrence, Al Pridham, H. O. Buckmann, O. F. Curtis, and Adrian Srb, molded us wet-behind-the-ears horticulturists into problem-solving, clear-thinking graduates. Their intelligent instruction was extraordinarily valuable and came at a time when I wanted with all my heart to absorb such material. But their instruction had no greater or lesser impact upon my horticultural life than the early lessons taught at the dinner table by my grandfather, father, and mother, and by Mr. Watts, Coot, and Wilbert in the fields at Lovejoy.

My accepted routine of studying all winter and working during the summer continued through my college years. After my freshman year I returned to the fields in Lovejoy, but I spent my second summer on a vegetable seed development farm in Connecticut. There were two groups of summer employees: college boys and girls from all over the East and local high school boys. I was glad I had spent my high school summers working in the nursery because my fellow college students were, for the most part, ill-prepared for all the hoeing and other menial labor we were required to do. They grumbled about the "damned high school" work, while I felt like Brer Rabbit in the briar patch. We were hand-pollinating corn and cucumbers to make unique genetic crosses — a fascinating new experience for me. Dr. Adrian Srb's fabulous genetics course the previous winter had whetted my appetite for more knowledge about hybridizing plants, and here I was in the middle of a commercial program to develop improved new varieties for farms and gardens.

Doodling roses prepared me well for our work in the cucumber field, since our job was to crawl down the row in the late afternoon and find any small female flowers that looked like they would open the next day. We would place a tiny clip on the flower to prevent it from opening and being pollinated by a wandering bee. We wanted to do our own pollinating so we would know exactly where the pollen came from.

The next morning we crawled down the row again, found the flowers we clipped the night before, found a male flower and dusted its pollen on the unclipped flower, reclipped it shut, then attached a white tag indicating it had been hand-pollinated. The manager explained that we were "selfing," which meant purifying that strain of cucumber. After a few days we crawled down the row once again and removed all the female flowers that hadn't been hand-pollinated. Of course we would then pitch the small fruit at whichever fellow worker's behind happened to be sticking up in the air most prominently. The gherkin with its spines was a favorite missile.

My experience in the Connecticut cucumber fields stood me in good stead many years later when I had a four-hour radio garden show on Saturday mornings in Atlanta. The purpose of the show was to solve gardening problems for listeners who called in, and the phone always rang off the hook when the first cucumber blossoms appeared. "What can I do to keep my cucumber blossoms from falling off? There are lots of blooms but I never get any fruit." I patiently explained that cucumbers, squash, zucchini, and melons were in a plant family that had male and female flowers. The male flowers appear before the female flowers and then fall off, so what was happening was perfectly natural. If it took more explanation to satisfy the caller, I would advise checking the blooms. "If you can see a tiny cucumber below the flower, you have found a female blossom, but if you don't see anything you have found a male flower," I would tell them.

Actually, cucumber flower questions were among my favorites. The answer made me sound smart and made the caller delighted that all was well in the cucumber patch.

That summer helped me understand how to survive Ithaca's cold winters: just remember how hot and miserable Connecticut was. Lovejoy was bad with its heat and gnats, but Connecticut, with its hot muggy air and mosquitoes big enough to drain a pint of blood with each bite, was ten times worse. Later I lived a hundred miles from the Equator while working on our project in Malaysia. After that one summer in Connecticut, the heat and humidity of the tropics didn't bother me at all.

H. O. Buckmann, the father of soil science, taught my Soil Science course the winter before my summer in Connecticut. He was one of those gifted teachers who could make the subject really come alive. For some reason, he took a liking to me and would often stop at my spot in the lab. He loved to kid me about being from the South and always called me "Rebel." As the term drew to a close, he stopped by and asked what I was going to do when I graduated. I said emphatically that I was going back to Georgia and enter the family company. He replied very seriously, "Don't do it, Rebel. The weather is too hot and the people of the South have always suffered because hot weather prevents the brain from working properly. You will never amount to anything if you go back to Georgia. You are a good student and can find a job up here where your brain will keep developing." For once in my life, I honestly didn't know what to say.

I did come back to Georgia and went to work for the company when I graduated from Cornell, but, with regard to my education, I continued to live under a lucky star. Nelson Crist, one of the South's greatest horticulturists, was still active in the company and took me under his wing.

The first week I was at work, Nelson pushed me into his car for a lesson on the unique trees of Atlanta. Nelson paid exclusive attention to plants along the road, entirely neglecting other motorists, but somehow we never hit anything. And once I had my nerves under control, I was fascinated by the trees he pointed out: a huge bald cypress growing out of a dry sidewalk in South Atlanta, a row of magnificent sycamore maples in front of a church in Ansley Park, the largest ginkgo in North Georgia growing on Peachtree Street, a huge American beech growing in Midtown where Indians used to camp, and a beautiful laburnum near where Turner Field now stands.

Nelson reserved Piedmont Park for our last stop since he had helped plan and plant the trees. I stood in awe of the magnificent row of European linden, the sugar maples, and best of all, the largest Red Horse chestnut I have ever seen in this part of the South. It wasn't our native red buckeye but an honest to goodness northern Red Horse chestnut. Nelson loved that tree and showed it with great pride since he had chosen it, then planted it many years before when he was with the parks department.

A year or so later on a Monday afternoon a pretty young woman came into the nursery with a flower in her hand. No one inside the store could identify it, so they sent her out to Nelson. She said nothing as she handed Nelson the flower.

"Young lady, what were you doing smooching with your boyfriend in Piedmont Park last night?" he asked with mock seriousness.

"How did you know that?" she cried.

"Simple. That is the flower of the only Red Horse chestnut in Atlanta. I planted it in Piedmont Park many years ago."

The redness in her face subsided as Nelson compli-
mented her for noticing such a beautiful tree, and she
departed a devoted tree lover.

I still give thanks for Nelson Crist for introducing me
to the magnificence of trees. To this day I believe trees are
God's most extraordinary plants, and no matter where I
go, I still love more than anything to discover a tree I've
never seen before.

~

Post-graduation

On one of his occasional evening visits on campus,
L. H. Bailey told us how he had planned his life: the first
twenty-five years in study, the second twenty-five years
in teaching, the third twenty-five years in writing, and
the last twenty-five years "doing as I damned please."

Though I cannot say my horticultural life has been as
well organized as Dr. Bailey's, mine has been strangely
varied and extremely interesting just the same. My first
twenty-one years were spent learning about growing
things from conversations at the dinner table, work in
the fields at Lovejoy, and finally at Cornell.

My next twenty-six years were spent in the seed and
nursery business where I honed and expanded my inter-

est in growing things, thanks in no small part to the horticulturists with whom I worked and to our customers, many of whom were expert gardeners.

It was also during this period that Betsy and I bought nineteen acres in then-rural Cherokee County north of Atlanta to live and raise our family. For the first time I was gardening in my own garden on my own land. My horticultural training was in ornamentals, but during my seed and nursery career I developed a deep interest in vegetables and fruits, and our vegetable garden at Sweet Apple was the highlight of summer. We grew sweet potatoes, which Wilbert and his crew came out to help me plant; peanuts so that our boys could discover their strange way of blooming in the top of the plant, then forming the nut underground; and the usual delicious Southern vegetables — tomatoes, eggplant, peppers, beans, cucumbers, squash, and zucchini, plus plenty of sweet corn.

While we were at it, we planted blueberries, figs, plums, apples, and pears, most of which are still with us even after our various extended stays overseas.

A gardener who never makes a mistake is no gardener at all. I have made my share, but I hope I've learned from each one. The biggest mess I ever made in my vegetable garden was when I planted Healing Squash. I had never heard of this plant until I saw a dried one hanging on the wall in the Reliance Fertilizer Company plant in Savannah. It was more like a gourd than a squash, with a hard brittle shell, and it was at least six feet long. The manager told me that it had been planted by the Salzburgers, who had come to Savannah in the early days but hadn't gotten along well with the English and so had moved inland, where they settled and began farming the land they cleared. They had brought from Austria many unique vegetables, which their descendants had continued to grow. One was Healing Squash, whose fresh fruit could be partially cut off for cooking, while leaving the remainder on the vine for dinner another day.

Upon hearing this wonderful story, I asked for some seed and planted it in a row near my usual crop of sweet corn, but I forgot to ask how much room they needed. My crop of Healing Squash grew down the rows, up in the sweet corn, out in the lawn, and over anything else in its way. I am sure it is a "half-acre plant," but I never really found out since those were the last Healing Squash I ever grew.

From the time I first fell in the fish pond and climbed the sweet gum tree at Lovejoy until now, I have been learning about growing things, and I hope I will never stop. One lesson I've surely learned is that success with plants comes more from experience than from adhering to strict rules. The more you garden, the more you understand how to grow things your way, not necessarily the "right" way. When we lived in Egypt, there was a highly advertised potato chip whose motto was, "Try it. You will adopt it." I like to apply that to gardening. If you're interested in a certain plant or technique, try it. If you're pleased with the result, adopt it.

Back to Dr. Bailey's time line: I spent my third period, some eighteen years, developing large commercial vegetable projects in far-off countries, an experience which gave me a completely different perspective on growing things, as well as deep understanding of people who belong to different races, cultures, and religions. Whatever the years to come may bring, I know my life will be focused on plants. I was born a horticulturist and will die one since "as a tree is bent, so will it grow."

Chapter Two

Red Clay Hills

Thus secure and tranquil, and meditating on the mar-
vellous scenes of primitive nature, as yet unmodified by
the hand of man, I gently descended the peaceful
stream on whose polished surface were depicted the
mutable shadows from its pensile banks; whilst myri-
ads of finny inhabitants sported in its pellucid floods.
— William Bartram, *Travels*, 1791

Before I was old enough to work in the fields, our family would sit on the front terrace as dusk came over the farm. After a hot summer day in Georgia, the coolness in the still evening air lies over you like a worn cotton sheet. It seemed like you could hear noises coming from miles away — people talking or singing or laughing. Each farm family's house had a black-iron wood-burning stove fueled by pieces of pine slabs, and you could hear the *chop* . . . *chop* of axes cutting firewood for cooking dinner. Soon the rich fragrance of those burning pieces of pine filled the air. The Chuck-Will's-Widow began its nightly ritual of calling for its mate. The happy laughter, axes chopping, pine fragrance, and the call of the Chuck-Will's-Widow are as real in my memories as they were on those nights.

Suddenly we would hear the clanking of trace chains as a line of mule-drawn wagons came across in front of us, slowly making their way beside the highway toward the barns after a day of cultivating Hastings Prolific Corn in the bottom lands north of the house. The rhythmic clanking of the traces was accompanied by the chanted songs that the field workers called hollers. Their work day was over and they would soon be home. I loved the sound of those wagons, but it was not until I worked in the fields that I could appreciate the pleasure of going home when the long day's work was done.

The best evening moments came after the field in front of the house was plowed and readied for planting. The soil was a dark chocolate brown instead of the more common bright red clay of most Georgia hill land, which had been worn out by planting cotton year after year. Our land was dark because it was rich and fertile, the result of my grandfather's and father's crop rotation and good plowing practices. Whenever I am near fertile, freshly plowed ground, with that rich aroma enveloping me, I still think of those evenings sitting on the porch at Lovejoy.

My grandfather's and father's interests in good soil management were more scientific and economic than my mother's. Land was dear to her, especially since her father had lost his land soon after the turn of the century. Her memories were of the sandy gray land of the upper Coastal Plains near Hawkinsville, Georgia, where she was born and had lived until she was my age as we sat on the terrace, but she had come to appreciate the soil of her adopted part of the state. The fragrance of the freshly plowed land in front of the house reached into all our hearts as the talk turned to practical matters like which cover crops were best and when it was wise to turn the land instead of merely disking it.

On those evenings of my boyhood, exactly what made our soil so rich and aromatic was not of much concern to me, but my level of interest rose dramatically when I became a part of the process of making soil produce crops. I became a constant and probably bothersome "why-asker" when I came home from the fields. I admit, though, that after fourteen hours of hard work and only a precious few hours before sunup, I don't think I was curious enough to remember any answers. I went to bed earlier and slept harder in those days than ever before or since.

The first time I remember being puzzled by a soil problem was one summer when I was fourteen. Every year Dad would go to Monticello, Florida, to inspect our watermelon contract crops. It was during the second summer I worked on the farm that he decided I should go with him to learn about the many kinds of watermelons and how they were grown under conditions different from those at Lovejoy. On the farm we mainly grew Stone Mountain, our own watermelon introduction, and contracted with Florida growers for most other cultivars. This prevented cross-pollination between our Stone Mountain and the other cultivars, which would have impaired the purity and quality of our seed.

Watermelons in those days were very susceptible to Fusarium Wilt disease, a soil fungus that could wipe out a crop planted where watermelons had been previously grown, so we drove miles upon miles to inspect fields planted on "new ground." I would walk with Dad through part of the field, then excuse myself and head for a fence where I could sit in the shade of a tree. After all, this was supposed to be a break from working in the hot sun at home.

After two or three of these excursions into the shade, it struck me how poor the crop was near the tree I was sitting under. The watermelon plants were weaker and weaker the closer to the tree they got, until the ground was bare and no plants survived under the tree's branches. I noticed that the fields near a pecan grove had the same problem. The closer the field was to a tree, the bigger the circle of poor growth was.

Not wanting to embarrass our contract grower by pointing out his poorly performing plants, I waited until our business was over and Dad and I were on the way home. I was fascinated to learn about the effect of tree root competition on crops, and my interest was finally whetted to the point that I began to stay up late enough to absorb some of the family discussions about the importance of soil quality.

Over time I developed the same appreciation of soil that my family shared. Momma would hold garden soil in her hand and make me smell its earthy fragrance while Dad and my grandfather talked about how the South's agricultural problems were rooted in one-crop cotton farming. In the 1920s my grandfather was among a group of agribusiness leaders who saw the disaster cotton was creating for Southern soils. The boll weevil had reached Georgia, causing huge cotton crop losses and devastating the South's economy. Something had to be done. My grandfather preached crop diversification —

planting corn and feed grain like wheat and oats instead of cotton.

In my young mind, unable to truly understand why fields of white bolls dominated our dinner-table conversation, cotton became evil incarnate. But slowly it began to sink in. Cotton was not really the villain; the problem was how and where it was grown. For me cotton became a valuable lesson about the life cycle of plants — from planting through harvest. Cotton simply took too long to mature in the uplands of the South. It had to be planted after the ground warmed in the spring, and it didn't mature until August and September. By the time hand-harvesting was over, it was too late to plant other crops which would be profitable to grow through the winter. When we took a trip in the fall or winter, Momma or Dad would point out fields of dead cotton plants standing like unworthy sentinels doing nothing to guard the land from erosion. A muddy creek or river nearby would be filled with a farmer's life-giving topsoil.

My grandfather promoted the use of cover crops to hold the topsoil in place during the winter. Crimson clover was his favorite because it could be planted in the fall as soon as cotton was harvested . . . if farmers could be convinced to change their ways. "These farmers are stubborn as Georgia mules," my grandfather would snort. But times were hard and there was precious little money from their cotton harvest to spend on a crop you couldn't eat. Many years passed before I would see a green field in the winter.

Agricultural practices began to change about the time I went to work in the fields, but change comes slowly in a farming community. Dad went out and bought the biggest tractor he could find because he wanted to plow the ground deeper than was possible with our standard cultivating tractors. All of us stood in awe of this huge machine that could drive a disk into the ground deeper than we ever saw. Of course, Dad had in mind not merely "disking" the ground deeply, but turning it. Living close to nature as they do, farmers have the habit of invoking the Lord to settle every issue. In the face of Dad's inclination to turn the soil, one of the managers said emphatically, "God Almighty put the topsoil on top and the subsoil on the bottom, and who are we to try to bring the subsoil up to the top and put the topsoil on the bottom?"

My father believed in compromise, something I had no interest in at that age. He bought the biggest disk he could find for our new tractor — one that would plow deeply without turning the soil — thereby preserving God's method of laying one layer of soil on another while accomplishing his purpose of cutting into the subsoil.

The traditionalists could find no heavenly invocations against subsoiling, a method of pulling a deep blade through a field at specific intervals. The idea was to break the "hardpan," the almost impervious layer of earth lying under the topsoil. Dad's theory was to open fissures in the "hardpan," which would let winter rains go deep into the ground rather than washing away the topsoil.

~

Rain

"Mr. H.G. shore talks about rain a lot," Coot would say and cackle in laughter. My grandfather quoted rainfall reports as often as the Bible. He kept up with rain surpluses and deficits more than stock market indexes.

My sister and I would laugh and say, "If Pa Pa had lived during Noah's time, he would insist there was a shortage of rain."

He also talked a lot about "moisture meeting." Merely raining wasn't always the answer. It was how much rain fell during a given period. He insisted that it took a long slow rain to fill up the topsoil and allow water to seep down to meet moisture in the subsoil, which he believed to be a great water reservoir. This water would be drawn up and become available to plants when it was dry, especially in May when young crops needed moisture to grow. I always enjoyed walking in the fields with him and watching him kick up soil with his toe to see how deeply it was darkened by moisture.

Yep, Mr. H. G. sure did talk about rain a lot.

All of us boys also liked rain. A heavy shower would let us leave the field, find a porch, and rest. The shower couldn't be too hard, though, or we would get "quartered" out. Each day was divided into quarters, and Mr. Watts had a big gold watch that he would extract from his pocket, checking to see if we had come to the end of one of these time periods. He kept his time book in his pocket and if it rained too hard he would send us home at a "quartering time." For the most part, we hated to be quartered out because it cut our pay, but we didn't always mind. The best of all worlds was to get quartered out after coming back from lunch. It would cost us a half day's pay, but we would have the afternoon off without having to go "to the house," where our mothers could always find something "useful" for us to do. We would hang around the shop talking nonsense with the blacksmith or go up to the barns to explore the lofts. Sometimes we would just lie on the fresh hay and talk while the rain pelted the tin roof over our heads.

Too much rain all at once could cause "washing," another soil problem aggravated by poor farming practices. When the topsoil was already soaked to capacity and the falling rain had no place to go, it ran on top of the ground in rivulets which would get deeper and deeper until they made a huge "wash" in the field. All of our rolling land was carefully terraced, with manmade ditches cutting across the fields at specific intervals to carry away excess rain. These were the same terraces where Momma and I found colonies of asparagus happily growing.

These terrace ditches were great fun to explore, by the way. During the last battles of the Atlanta campaign in the War Between the States, the Yankees and "our side" had a big battle on our farm. The Yankees were trying to cut the railroad that ran in front of the house and right through the middle of the farm. Some of the terraces that we still used, especially around our house, were originally dug by one side or the other to be used as trenches during this long drawn-out battle.

This bit of history had interesting consequences when I was growing up. To begin with, there were the ghosts of soldiers killed during the battle. At particular places around the farm, these ghosts (or "haints," as they were called) would plague farm workers who happened to walk by as darkness fell. One of these haunted locations was between our house and Willie Pine's, and when dinner ran late, Dad would lend either Willie or Ludie, his wife, a big flashlight to shine on the ghosts to scare them away.

Another serious problem was the number of unex-
ploded artillery shells that were plowed up. One farm
wife, needing something to chock her black iron wash
pot, found what she thought was a rock in the adjacent
field and stuck it under the pot in place of a missing foot.
Unfortunately it was an artillery shell. When she lit the
fire to boil her family's clothes, the shell exploded and
injured her severely. Dad had to constantly warn everybody to stay away from these shells that had been left
behind seventy-five years earlier.

The good part of having had the battle on the farm
was the number of bullets we could find in the field in
front of the house and across the railroad on Bullet Hill.
You could easily find them after a heavy rain since they
were made of lead and remained on top of little pillars of
soil after the surrounding soil washed away. This was fine
for me at the time because I loved to collect these arti-
facts, but it took a Soil Science course at Cornell for me
to realize that this indicated how much undetected washing occurs in a field.

Dad discovered a wealth of information in the reprints
of William Bartram's *Travels*, which was published in
1791 and describes Bartram's journeys through Georgia,
Florida, Alabama, and the Carolinas. He was fascinated,
as I have become in later years, at the beautiful descrip-
tions of the way the land looked before our European

ancestors spread inward and developed their farms. Bartram found pristine rivers and open land covered with vegetation. Once Dad and I were driving through southeast Georgia when we crossed the Altamaha River after a rainy spell. The water was red with Georgia topsoil. He urged me to read Bartram's description of the same river before farms were developed along its banks. Bartram described how he could see fish swimming far below the surface. "See what we have done to the land. That's why crops do so poorly. All the rich topsoil is washing away," Dad moaned. I began to understand why soil was so important to my family and to our farm.

~

Foreign Soil

Working on our overseas projects was a "continuing education" course in soil management. I remember how delighted my father was to hear about the 3,000-acre vegetable farm I helped develop in Southeast Asia. He wanted the details about what the land was like, how we plowed and cultivated, and how we kept the humus content high enough for good production in a place where the year-round growing season rapidly destroyed organic matter.

Our practices were not too different from those Dad used at Lovejoy, except that our John Deere field-prep tractor was about ten times larger than the big Farmall he had bought for the farm many years ago. He couldn't believe we had a tractor that pulled a three-shank sub-soiler with meter-long tines as deep as they would go and was so large that it was hinged in the middle in order to make turns at the end of a row. Our big tractor at Lovejoy when I was a boy had a tough time pulling a one-shank subsoiler half that deep in the ground. But the principle was the same.

In Malaysia we had a calcareous (chalky) hardpan which acted much like the clay hardpan we had at Lovejoy, preventing heavy rains from moving downward into that subsoil holding tank my grandfather always talked about. Dad couldn't believe our rainfall might be five inches or more in an afternoon. "Pa [that's what he called my grandfather] might even think that's enough for the moisture to meet," Dad said with a chuckle.

I think he was most proud of my efforts in Malaysia when he asked about the use of cover crops to build the soil by adding humus. "In all that heat and with such a long growing season, you are going to need a lot of humus in the soil," he stated very bluntly. I was prepared for the question and enjoyed telling him that I had dis-covered a legume called mung beans, which made an excellent cover and soil-building crop in a place where clovers wouldn't grow well. Mung beans even produced the needed nitrogen just like clover did. That pleased him greatly.

Our agricultural project in Egypt introduced me to sandy soil for the first time in my horticultural career. The project was outside the Nile delta in reclaimed desert land that had not been farmed since the time of Cleopatra. My partner, Bill Evans, called our farm the largest sandbox in the world. Our workers at Lovejoy would have called it "po' land."

The Egyptian method of reclaiming land was to build canals to take water to a given farm. The process did not include any soil improvement except the construction of drainage ditches to take away excess irrigation water. This prevented water from going down into the soil, then moving up to the surface again where it would quickly evaporate and leave behind a damaging crust of calcium and other salts. Good drainage was a necessity. We also employed the same large tractors we later used in Malaysia so that we could open the subsoil of the fields — another safeguard against crusting.

Our first crops were disappointing, far below my expectations. Our first farm manager was a modernist, and though his technical staff used all sorts of meters and instruments to test moisture concentration as well as nutrient levels, crops grew poorly. Fortunately, we replaced him with a true farmer who grew things "by the seat of his pants." John took one look at the fields, then toured the area for a source of humus. He found a huge chicken producer and immediately began a program of applying as much as fifteen tons of chicken manure per acre. Within seven months we were harvesting over two million pounds of tomatoes and one million pounds of cantaloupes per month.

John was a strict disciplinarian whose demands were aimed at producing good crops, a priority that often came into conflict with some of our own American staff as well as the Egyptian agricultural graduates. The young educated types — both American and Egyptian — wanted to follow the rules and didn't mind arguing with John, who was only a high school graduate but who, in my book, had a Ph.D. in agriculture from his thirty-five years of experience.

I was riding with John through a field of tomatoes divided into four blocks when the Egyptian irrigation supervisor rapidly approached in his truck.

"Mr. John, we are getting tip-wilt in the tomatoes, " he cried out anxiously.

"What is your water schedule," John asked.

"Six hours in each block," he replied — the maximum amount since there were four blocks to be irrigated from one pumping system during a twenty-four-hour period.

"Go to eight hours per block," John replied.

The graduate started toward his truck, then whirled around and cried out, "But Mr. John, how can we do that when there are only twenty-four hours in a day."

John replied gruffly, "I'm just a high school graduate. You graduated from college, so you figure it out."

The young man looked upset at first but quickly realized John was making the point that he must maximize every minute and be sure all pumps were in order and really pumping twenty-four hours per day. Agricultural rules are like statistics. They may help, but they don't take the place of common sense.

In Egypt, just as in the Lovejoy of my boyhood, change comes slowly to the farm. I remember the frustration of my friend Dr. Yussef Wali, Egypt's Minister of Agriculture and inner cabinet minister for President Hosni Mubarak. He was extremely knowledgeable and stood out as a high-ranking public servant who was truly dedicated to his work, but he was handcuffed by a system long out of date.

"Our problem is that the good land in the delta was divided into ten-acre holdings by the socialists under President Nassar," he explained one day when I was in his office in Cairo. "No one can afford to buy a tractor, so we must use the animals to work the fields and also to turn the water wheels for irrigation. It takes 50 percent of the land to produce food for the animals needed to produce crops. If we had larger holdings and tractors, we could double production immediately by using all the land for food crops instead of half to produce animal food."

All of our overseas experiences were memorable and deeply enlightening. I learned a tremendous amount, and, despite various language barriers, I hope that I did some teaching as well. I remember being asked to make a talk in Surabaya, Indonesia, about how we developed land in Malaysia. My audience was delighted to learn that Cornell was my university, since Cornell had trained a tremendous number of students from foreign countries and was well recognized in every country I had been in. "Did you use H. O. Buckmann's *Nature and Properties of Soil*?" one person asked. When I replied that I had taken Dr. Buckmann's course, you would have thought I had won a Nobel Prize by the awe and respect bestowed upon me.

Tropical soil is like the Georgia red clay I grew up with — low in organic matter after several years of constant cropping. So I was extolling the virtues of manure when I suddenly realized that every time I said the word manure, my translator said "poo-poo." I had a hard time continuing, since I was trying not to laugh and at the same time thinking that surely Indonesia had a better word for manure, but I managed to plow on through. After the program I found out that, sure enough, "poopoo" was the word for manure in Bahasa, Indonesia's language. Some things, like soil, are universal.

~

Heritage

My grandfather died in 1962, for which, in a way, I am thankful. The South's population had not yet begun to explode. Bulldozers weren't rampantly scraping away the topsoil which he fought so hard to help farmers rebuild after cotton farming ruined it. If he were alive now and at the age when he fought against one-crop cotton farming, I am sure he would be at the forefront of the battle against the wanton soil destruction of developers. His methods would include educating developers to be responsible citizens and convincing homeowners of the importance of buying homes from developers who protect the land.

My father lived long enough to see the bulldozers do their work, and before his death in 1991, he and I spent many hours commiserating over the problems facing gardeners in all the new subdivisions. "I think it's sinful the way the developers build houses these days. They flatten the land, remove all the trees, and push the topsoil into the low spots. Nobody can grow anything without topsoil," he pontificated. I agreed with all my heart. We were walking the same path when I told him I believed that a bulldozer ruined more soil in an hour than cotton did in fifty years. He loved that.

Dad liked to say, "You should start every gardening project on your knees." Then he would explain how important it was to inspect the soil by getting on your knees and feeling it, then preparing it properly before planting regardless of whether you were planting trees, shrubs, annuals, or vegetables.

In 1967, a new radio station, WRNG, started in Atlanta with an all-talk format. One of the features each morning was "Call Kate," a call-in show hosted by a delightful lady named Kate Bankston. Kate called just before the station went on the air to ask if I would join her to answer gardening questions. I agreed to, and that Monday morning program began fourteen years of continuous weekly appearances, most of them after Kate had moved on. During all those years, I seldom had a time when no one was waiting to get on the air. In fact, our gardening program was so popular that it almost went to my head, but then I saw Santa Claus's numbers.

As I think back, a remarkable percentage of the questions people asked over those many years had to do with soil-related problems. One fall morning a man called to ask about preparing his bulldozed, light-red-clay front yard for planting grass. He didn't have a tiller and didn't want to use peat moss because it was expensive, so I suggested scratching up the soil, then planting crimson clover over the winter. In the spring he could work the clover into the ground with a rented tiller and plant grass. I had him sold until he asked about cutting the clover. I told him not to cut it but let it grow.

"Hell," he replied, "that's crazy. My wife wants a lawn so I'm going to just sow seed and put on some fertilizer." I have often wondered how many people like him have taken the easy route and how much money for seed and fertilizer they have spent without ever having a nice lawn. Sometimes I am tempted to say, "Forget about grass. Have bare ground that you can sweep clean with a yard broom like people in the country used to." But I never do.

At Sweet Apple, we have red clay soil, former cotton land, and over the years I have tried just about everything to improve it. We built compost heaps, used our horses' manure, planted cover crops, and tilled in peat moss, ground bark, and any other new or rediscovered materials. I've found cover crops to be the most effective overall, though I use a combination of peat moss and perlite in Betsy's flower beds since she isn't too keen about crimson clover or Austrian winter peas growing there during the winter.

I grew up using German peat moss, but when the bogs in East Germany were under Soviet control, that product became scarce. Now I use Canadian peat moss exclusively. I had a brief affair with ground bark, which is very popular with growers and homeowners because it is cheap. But the day I looked out and for the first time in twenty-five years saw annuals dying with Pythium and Fusarium diseases, I decided bark was no good and returned to my old favorite. My disease problems vanished.

I plant crimson clover in my vegetable garden each fall to add humus and nitrogen and to prevent erosion during the winter. My grandfather was right; crimson clover is a great cure for cotton land's problems, but it does have one drawback. We get a wonderful man, George Waters, to bush hog the pasture two or three times a year. Up in his eighties now, he has more good information and the best common sense of anybody around. One late-fall afternoon, Mr. Waters took a look at the beautiful, succulent crimson clover we had covering the vegetable garden and said, "You sure are in for deer problems this winter."

I had never given it a thought, but Mr. Waters was right. Those deer ate up our clover. But don't worry. If you think you might have a problem with deer eating up the cover crop on your vegetable garden, you can do what we did — get a big dog.

Everyday I see soil being ruined and I fear for the future. Government rules aren't the answer since government road and construction projects are as bad as developers in destroying the land, along with nearby streams and rivers. Cost effectiveness is more important than survival.

My son Chris recently returned to Cornell to earn a master's degree in horticulture. He is learning some revolutionary theories on planting. The new guidelines advise little if any soil preparation beyond the extent of the plant's ball of earth. "They are teaching that trees do not have nearly as deep or wide a root system as originally thought," he told me.

I just laughed. "Remember those trees you cut up for the lady up the road after Hurricane Opal and how you tried to winch the stumps back into the holes? Those trees had roots much farther out than Cornell is teaching."

"They sure did," he agreed, thinking back on that backbreaking work.

I also remembered the watermelon fields planted next to those pecan trees in Florida when I was a young boy.

The decline in vigor of the watermelon plants indicated pretty clearly just how far out those tree roots extended.

A lifetime of experience has made me reluctant to feverishly embrace new ideas. I say, try anything once, and if it doesn't work discard it. That's the one rule I insist on.

One of my best friends when growing up was M. H. Elder, Jr., whose father had a huge red clay farm west of Lovejoy. M. H., Sr., and Dad were close friends just as "Brother" and I were. M. H. and his wife were at our house for a party one day when M. H. sang out in a loud voice, "Don, remember when I asked you about planting peanuts on the farm? You said forget it since peanuts needed sandy soil. Well, I didn't take your advice and planted them anyway. I made more money off those peanuts than any crop I ever planted."

Dad was flabbergasted. He told me many times since that he never could understand how M. H. made such a big crop of peanuts on red clay cotton land. "I guess he didn't know any better, so he produced a good crop anyway," Dad said, using one of his favorite expressions.

Farming and gardening are not exact sciences. Experience is worth a whole lot more than methodology. Science points out the direction of the rows, but the farmer or gardener has to plow the rows, plant the crop, and grow it to maturity. He'll need all the help he can get, but the most help of all is likely to be the lessons he's learned in the past.

The gardener's number-one priority is to provide ideal conditions for plants to grow in. Insects and diseases will certainly play their part, but we must grow plants well before being concerned about the varieties of pestilence. In all the places I have grown plants, good soil is the key to good production. All other problems are secondary.

Dad was right: "Start every gardening project on your knees."

Chapter Three

Entering the Plant Kingdom

What's in a name?
— Shakespeare

I learned to grow plants when I was very young but didn't truly appreciate them until much later. In my days in the nursery fields, I learned what I didn't like — junipers and okra, for example — before I learned what I liked. Except for my climbing trees — sweet gum and chinaberry — the plants in the woods and around the house, as well as in Momma's garden, meant little to me when I was a child.

I envy people who have sudden and profound revelations because I have never been blessed with any. My changes come slowly, sometimes very slowly. When I graduated from high school, I could appreciate Momma's garden, but I can't say that I had deep feelings for the plants she grew. I could identify many as we walked around and she talked about why she used this one or that one in a certain place. But they were merely images on her canvas. She painted the picture; I did not. It was her work of art, not mine.

During my first two years at Cornell, I learned the scientific principles that govern the plant kingdom. Botany gave the basics. Plant physiology, genetics, and plant taxonomy expanded the basics into more detailed understanding of plants and plant processes. I learned identification and how to key a plant's place in the plant kingdom while studying plant taxonomy under Dr. George Lawrence. I studied the way moisture moved up the trunk of a hundred-foot tree under Dr. O. F. Curtis in plant physiology. Dr. Adrian Srb taught us the way genetics works in plant evolution. We counted fruit flies late at night to understand the principles he presented in class. But I experienced no sudden affinity for individual plants.

The closest I came to developing a personal feeling for a maple, yew, or any other plant was in a course on basic woody plant material taught by Dr. John Cornman. He took us to the Cornell Plantations, a large farm Dr. Bailey had given to the university for an arboretum, to see one of his favorite trees.

"You will seldom see a tree with such spectacular fall color," he told us as we unloaded from the vans. I guess my mind was somewhere else since I missed the name of the tree he was so excited about. We walked across a grassy meadow to a small hill on which was a scrawny but brilliantly colored tree. We stood looking as he extolled its virtues in glowing terms. It was a sweet gum, my sweet gum, the same kind of tree I loved to climb when I was a boy. Dr. Cornman explained that sweet gums shouldn't grow at Ithaca's latitude and in its intense cold. "Isn't it beautiful!" he exclaimed with obvious delight.

I wanted to say, "It is so scrawny. You should see the one in our backyard at home." But I didn't. I had been taught not to "take the wind out of someone's sail." At any rate, maybe because we were both foreigners in an alien land, I did develop a fondness for that pitiful little sweet gum.

My appreciation and love for plants began in those classes and slowly grew over the years, guiding me into my career as a horticulturist and a gardener. Dr. Cornman showed me how to see plants as more than mere objects in a landscape or garden.

His advanced woody plant material course, which I took the fall of my senior year, was my favorite of all the classes at Cornell. Just a handful of upperclassmen and graduate students could get in, and there was very little classroom work. Dr. Cornman wanted us to see plants growing naturally or being used in the landscape, so instead of studying slides, we drove around the Ithaca area looking at and learning about trees and shrubs. The finale was a trip to Washington, D.C., Longwood Gardens in Delaware, and the Morris Arboretum near Philadelphia. We piled into a big van and spent three days on the road in search of plants not seen in Ithaca's cold climate.

Our first stop was the Bishop's Garden at the Washington National Cathedral. We walked through the garden speaking in low reverent voices like we did inside the great cathedral with its beautiful carvings and stained-glass windows. This was my first experience with man's historical goal of creating a *paradeisos* on earth, and the Bishop's Garden, with its huge boxwood borders and pansies as colorful as the stained glass, was a heavenly place of peace and quiet amidst the turmoil of our nation's capital.

We also drove around Washington looking at special plants Dr. Cornman had found on previous excursions. Being the only Southerner in the group, I was kidded a lot about my accent and homeland, so I was always looking for a chance to strike a blow in my (and the South's) defense. Dr. Cornman, who was a master at suspense, made us learn by deduction. We came to one of Washington's many squares, the one with a statue of General Phil Sheridan on his horse. After we had circled the square a few times, an awful smell began to pour into the van, eliciting strong complaints from the group.

"What do you smell?" Dr. Cornman asked.

"A Yankee general," I replied before anyone else could answer.

Everyone burst into laughter and gave me hell, while Dr. Cornman made another trip around the square to emphasize his point. "It is *not* Phil Sheridan. It is the fruit of the ginkgo," he solemnly declared while stopping the van to let us out. The smell was like rancid butter and almost made us sick as we stood on the sidewalk looking down at smashed ginkgo fruit all over the street.

Dr. Cornman had explained the problem in class, but having never experienced the awful smell, we didn't believe it could be so bad. I learned that day never to plant two ginkgo trees close together, or you might have a yard filled with rancid-smelling fruit each fall. If your ginkgo tree is a male, it can't set fruit. If it's a female without a male nearby, it won't set fruit. In those days, all ginkgo trees were grown from seed, so there was a fifty-fifty chance any tree could be male or female. Now, of course, the wary shopper can buy grafted male ginkgo trees and eliminate the risk of a foul harvest.

~

Size Matters

Each plant has its own character. It may have wonderful structure, beautiful flowers, intense fragrance, or some other unique quality. One thing it will certainly have is its own optimum size, which you'll want to be aware of when you are planning and planting.

I think the southern magnolia, *Magnolia grandiflora*, is the most beautiful of all evergreen trees. I have several that are forty or fifty feet tall with lower branches sweeping the ground. I define the fragrance of their blossoms as something that smells like lemonade tastes. Huge, squawking pileated woodpeckers come each fall to gorge themselves on the red fruit, then provide an extra blessing by spreading expelled seeds all over our woods, in which magnolia seedlings now proliferate. We don't have as many magnolias growing on our twenty acres as we have seedling pines, but we have plenty. And magnolias don't get borers like the pines. Maybe nature is working to rid us of pines in favor of magnolias, which are longer-lasting and much more beautiful.

Magnolias offer a great example of the foresight necessary when planning a landscape. Espaliers were extremely popular during my nursery days, and a local landscape designer decided that *Magnolia grandiflora* would make an excellent espalier against a large brick wall. Several were planted on the walls of Atlanta's old St. Joseph's Infirmary, as well as on the side of the administration building of the Atlantic Steel Company. The magnolias were attractive for a few years, with their carefully pruned limbs attached to the red brick walls in a perfect fan. The green leaves muted the barren look of the large walls and produced an appealing contrast. Unfortunately, the magnolias grew larger and larger until drastic yearly pruning was necessary. The first part of the summer they looked bare and ugly, in the middle of the summer they were fine, but by the end of the summer they were overgrown and unattractive. Ultimately, the ones at St. Joseph's damaged the walls and had to be removed. At Atlantic Steel, the landscapers stopped pruning the trees and left them to become awkward-looking monsters kissing but not holding the wall.

The problem is also illustrated by the story of a friend of mine who lived in a beautiful in-town subdivision. The neighborhood was filled with nicely landscaped, expensive homes, but I could not believe how close to the houses and to each other the trees had been planted. My friend's house was about fifty feet from the street, and his relatively small front yard was planted with four trees — two magnolias close to the street and two water oaks between them and the house. These fast-growing trees were quickly becoming too much for the yard.

"How should I prune them to keep them in bounds?" he asked.

"You can't," I replied. "If you prune either a magnolia or water oak you will ruin its shape. I suggest you prune the water oaks with a chain saw at the ground."

Of course, this just made him mad, and he never did anything. Some years after he died, I drove by his house, and the front yard was an ugly jungle.

Landscape designers defend such choices by blaming the client's demand for instant maturity. One very fine landscape architect explained this practice: "I know better and try to discourage people from setting large plants too close together, but they don't want to wait several years for them to develop. My clients tell me they will move before well-spaced plants look good." The subsequent owners have to deal with problems caused by overplanting.

Each type of plant has its own growth habit and mature size. A major part of enjoying a plant is understanding its characteristics so you can use it wisely. My mother constantly complained about her abelia hedge. "If I had known what it was going to be like, I certainly wouldn't have planted it," she told us over and over. She wanted an evergreen hedge to surround one of the terraced gardens and planted abelias because they were not only evergreen but also produced attractive blossoms. Unfortunately, the abelia hedge dropped most of its foliage during cold winters when winds swept across the big field in front of the house. Momma never removed the hedge, though; she discovered that the birds would solve her problem by seeding cherry laurels among the abelias. She encouraged the seedlings to grow and become the evergreen part of her hedge. "There's more than one way to skin a cat," she said.

Trees are the hardest plant to choose and place correctly in a landscape. Whenever I showed customers at our nursery our largest trees, they would invariably say, "Those trees are so small. They will never do anything." I would explain growth rates and expectations, only to hear the insistent reply, "I want a *fast*-growing tree. One that will give me shade this summer." My lecture about the problems associated with fast-growing trees — weak wood, sparse growth, messy fruits — fell on deaf ears. Many customers left without buying a tree, then returned later to tell us about a miracle tree they purchased through an advertisement or catalog. "It grows six feet or more a year," they would brag. Few lived in a house long enough for weak wood problems to present themselves; the subsequent owners would bear the expense of buying replacements.

We employed neighborhood high school boys on the

weekends to load plants and do all the other heavy lifting for our customers. One of these fine young men (whose older brother had also worked for us) helped us solve an interesting tree problem. A customer came in asking about a terrible disease on his maple tree.

"It has long strands of white fungus hanging down from the leaves," he said.

None of us had any idea what the problem was, and the customer left without having been helped at all. Milton Nardin, the nursery manager, looked in book after book and asked all the rest of us, including Charles Hudson, the garden center manager and a horticultural authority. No one noticed the neighborhood boy listening intently. After lunch, he returned with a handful of silver maple leaves.

"We have that problem, too," he exclaimed. The problem wasn't a fungus but a terrible insect like a woolly aphid that attaches itself to the underside of the leaves. "And it drips on anything underneath," Jimmy said. Several of us walked down the street to Jimmy's house and observed, first hand, the awful problem.

"Dad went to your nursery when we first moved in and asked about a fast-growing tree, but you didn't have one fast enough for him, so he went to another nursery and bought this silver maple. He sure is sorry he did," Jimmy said. Unfortunately, plant dealers sometimes fail to observe plants long enough to understand their mature characteristics prior to listing them, so buyers can be led astray. On the other hand, nurserymen I know and respect feel a strong obligation to recommend the best plant for a situation even when it conflicts with a home-owner's choice.

After attending a funeral at Westview Cemetery in Atlanta, Dad took me to see what he called "the original Burford holly." It was huge, standing twenty-five feet high and almost that wide, and it completely changed my attitude about planting Burford holly. Momma's eight-foot-tall hedge had formed my vision of a Burford holly until I saw the original plant, but now I realized that this plant was often being confined to overly cramped quarters. When we opened the Cheshire Bridge Road Garden Center, we planted several of the new Dwarf Burford holly but soon realized the term "dwarf" was relative to the original Burford holly at Westview Cemetery, not to three-foot-high windows. Over the years before we sold the company, we made it a practice of planting as many new introductions as possible on the grounds of all our garden centers to show customers how a plant looked as it matured.

I also had an interesting experience with the 'Nellie R. Stevens,' one of the most beautiful of all hollies. When it was first introduced, I noticed the decidedly upright growth, with shoots that made it look like it wanted to be a tree, not a shrub. Consequently, I got in a terrible argument with a grower who was selling heavily pruned plants in one- and two-gallon containers. He insisted they would make excellent foundation plants, but I was convinced they would be a mess in restricted places. After we sold the company and I had much more time to observe plants growing in various environments, I found a beautiful 'Nellie R. Stevens' growing next to a tall brick wall in a shopping center. It had a perfect pyramid shape and was taller than the large wall — hardly the ideal foundation plant.

Dr. Cornman taught us to classify plant heights into rough categories: under waist height, waist height to eye level, and above eye level, which is an excellent way to choose the best plant for a particular place in the landscape. However, plant size may vary from location to location as well as according to how they are planted and cared for. I planted Carissa holly when it was first introduced as a low-growing holly for foundation plantings, especially under low windows. It seemed perfect for a spot in front of my house. Now that they are almost twenty-five years old, I realize that I should have planted them at least five feet apart rather than the customary three feet. Instead of spreading into large mounds, they have grown together and up into my windows five feet above the ground. Spaced farther apart, these plants would have remained lower and would have looked much better than mine do now.

Of course, you can inhibit a plant's growth by taking poor care of it, but the result is usually an unattractive plant. A good maintenance program with slow-release fertilizer offers the best of all worlds — attractive plants that grow to their natural size.

~

Names Matter, Too

One day after Betsy and I were engaged, she said, "Since I'm going to be the wife of a horticulturist, I need to know some botanical names to fit my new role. Teach me a real hard name to start with." I chose *Metasequoia gliptostroboides*, the botanical name for dawn redwood. She quickly conquered the long Latin binomial, but if she hadn't, it wouldn't have mattered since she said "ca-meel-lia," not "ca-mel-lia," and pronounced "tomato" with a Virginia broad "a." She also brought a whole new dimension to our family's use of botanical names. She could spell them, which is something horticulturists are not particularly good at.

Growing up in Lovejoy, my sister and I knew plants

pretty well for youngsters. We hid in the *abelia* hedge or among the *boxwood*. We made people out of *wisteria* pods, not just pods. I didn't climb just any old tree; I climbed a *sweet gum* tree. My sister and I were not allowed to go closer to the highway than the *chinaberry* tree, which was about halfway out the driveway. When we visited my grandmother Hastings, I wanted to climb the *mimosa* tree. My mother and father constantly called plants by their botanical names since they felt you insulted a plant when you didn't call it by its correct name.

Being so focused on plants and their names had its disadvantage. On a trip through Central Florida, as we approached Cypress Gardens we began to see Burma Shave–type signs: "It's Azalea Time in Cypress Gardens," read the first one; followed by, "It's Hibiscus Time in Cypress Gardens"; and then, "It's Camellia Time in Cypress Gardens." Mother or Dad would usually have some comment to make, but when we passed a sign which read, "It's Camera Time in Cypress Gardens," there was a long silence from the front seat. Finally Dad asked, "What's a ca-meer-a?" Momma responded with a gale of laughter before managing to choke out, "That's something you take a picture with."

Since my mother loved camellias and had a fine collection of them in the garden, she frequently attended well-known camellia shows throughout the South. One year she took me to one of the largest, held in Augusta, Georgia. The grande dame of the camellia world was an ancient and formidable lady named Mrs. Sheffield Phelps, who was seated on the stage of the auditorium like the Queen of England. I was about eleven at the time and shyly approached Mrs. Phelps to be introduced. Momma had instructed me to be extra polite and to be sure to say how much I liked camellias. When I shook Mrs. Phelps's hand, I mumbled something about liking "ca-MEL-lias." She looked at me sternly and huffed, "Don't be fancy with me, boy; say it right. It is *never* 'ca-MEL-lia.' It is 'ca-MEEL-lia.' Remember that, boy." I was thoroughly embarrassed, and the thing was, I will never know why I said it wrong. Everybody in our household pronounced it just like Mrs. Phelps did. I must have been unconsciously rebelling against her *hauteur*.

Working in the nursery wasn't the best way for me to learn proper pronunciation of botanical names since the variety of Georgia dialects spoken on the farm really butchered the Latin. Common names were written the way they sounded, and most names were shortened — like *Rosa multiflora* to just *multiflora*. But the whole Latin grouping was attempted on occasion. I would laugh and laugh at Coot when he tried to say the botanical name for an *Arborvitae*. "It's a *Thuja orientalis bonita aurea nana,*" he would say with a South Georgia twang which obliterated the Latin pronunciation. I was never devilish enough to tell him when the name was changed to *Platycladus orientalis bonita* with the *aurea nana* dropped, even though I really wanted to hear him pronounce *Platycladus.*

Plants do need universal botanical names. I was constantly getting mixed up at Cornell because common names in the South were so different from common names in the North. And in my work overseas, I have found the use of common names to be impossible. In the Philippines, the common tropical hibiscus is called *Gomamela* in Manila, and everything from *Atoanga* to *Taukangga* outside Manila. Worse, sometimes even common names were unavailable. When I first arrived in Malaysia to develop a farming project, I had never seen such magnificent trees, some of which were so big that a single log filled a large truck. I wanted to know the names of those magnificent specimens, so I asked Loi Teh Ong, our administrative manager. After ignoring me as long as he could, he finally said with exasperation, "It's a wild tree!"

Dr. George Lawrence's course in taxonomy at Cornell finally made sense and order out of botanical classification and naming. Each plant has at least two parts to its name, like we have a first name and a last name. The first name is the genus, the second is the species. In the plant world my name would be Hastings Don, like Chinese names, not Don Hastings like we use in the Western world. Even so, botanical names often change as the International Committee on Nomenclature tries to sort out *which* botanical name is correct. The theory is simple. The name assigned by the plant's discoverer is the precedent name, that is if there are no complications, like when the discoverer assigns a name that's botanically wrong. The genus has to be botanically correct, which simply means you can't have a plant called *Thuja*, like Coot did, when botanically it belongs to the *Platycladus* genus.

"How would you like to be called by the wrong name?" Dad would ask when I moaned about plant names being so complicated.

Of course, we had countless plant name problems in our catalog business. One of our order writers showed me a request that said, "Please send me 1 Maglionola Flyscatter and bill me for the cost if it ain't too much." None of the order writers had the faintest idea what plant she was asking for. I tried and tried to figure out the name using phonics. Suddenly it came to me that she wanted a *Magnolia fuscata* — called banana shrub in the South — an evergreen with small yellow flowers shaped like and smelling like bananas. Actually the correct name was *Michelia fuscata*, but I wasn't going to confuse our good customer since its earlier name had indeed been *Magnolia fuscata*.

The name problem is often compounded by people's memories. Marechal Neil was a favorite Southern rose in earlier days, but rarely grown by the time I entered the business. It was known for its heavy flowering habit and pleasing fragrance. We had so many requests for Marechal Neil roses that Dad found a grower who propagated them and made arrangements for enough to supply us for the catalog.

Listing the Marechal Neil rose was a disaster. When people saw we had them in the catalog, they ordered them like crazy, but a year later the complaints started rolling in. "You sent me the wrong plant," customer after customer reported, usually adding that the blooms were smaller than the ones they had grown up with. Many noted also that ours weren't fragrant enough. Dad went to the grower's fields and inspected the Marechal Neil flowers, which were exactly like those Dad was familiar with.

"Let's don't list Marechal Neil next year," he told me. "People remember them from their younger days, and everything from your youth gets bigger and better the older you get." Now that I am of the older generation I realize just how right he was.   Back in my mail order days, we were always receiving letters or calls from people who either had a rare plant (they thought) or had found one in the woods. If the writer was convincing enough, either Dad or I would investigate to see for ourselves whether the plant was unique enough to propagate.

One time Dad received a letter from a man at the foot of Pine Mountain in Georgia describing, with some excitement, a rare dogwood he had found in the woods nearby — a dogwood that bloomed in the summer. Of course, Dad had to drive to Pine Mountain to see for himself, but when he saw the few small, blooming plants growing in containers in the man's yard, he realized immediately that they were not dogwoods but *Stewartia malacodendron*, a rarely seen native plant. He also made the mistake of telling the man what the plant actually was. Dad wanted to see a specimen of *Stewartia malacodendron* growing in the wild, but when he asked the man to take him up the mountain to the mother plant, the old fellow refused.

"I ain't fixin' to show you where the mother plant is," he said, "'cause all you want to do is steal my summer-flowering dogwood."

Too bad. If the fellow had been convinced to propagate his *Stewartia*, we could have sold a lot of them.

I hated it when Mrs. Phelps called me "boy." We all like to be called by our names, and I can't help but think that plants do, too. My climbing tree was a sweet gum when I was young and a *Liquidamber styraciflua* when I became a horticulturist. Both names made my tree a friend whom I could identify and feel close to. I have roses in my garden that were sent by large rose nurseries for me to try. Growing next to my 'Harry G. Hastings' — a rose I found and named for my grandfather — is a beautiful pink variety that has only a number for identification. Without its proper name, this forlorn beauty seems to me like a convict in a prison.

~

Associations

I like some plants because I associate them with people who mean something to me or places that I have visited and enjoyed. Connecting plants with places or people is one way I have expanded my interest in growing things.

I never look at a white dogwood without remembering how much dogwoods meant to my mother. She felt they were almost sacred, not because of the Passion story told about them, but because they are so special in the South. She was as angry as I ever saw her when Dad came home one night and told us someone had cut a number of dogwoods in the most spectacular grove on the farm. "Why?" she asked angrily.

"They use dogwood to make spindles for looms in cotton mills because the wood is so dense and hard," Dad explained. "It's hard to find and brings a lot of money."

"He had better not come over here and cut any dogwoods in my garden or woods," she exclaimed. She didn't say exactly what would happen, but I knew there would be hell to pay.

Henry Chase, the famous Huntsville, Alabama, nurseryman, showed me several special dogwoods in his nursery that had spectacular blossoms. He sold one to Wayside Nursery, who introduced it as 'White Cloud' dogwood. Another, the best I thought, he saved to patent and introduce himself. But he couldn't think of a name that really suited this beautiful plant. Henry and I were sitting in a hotel room at a nurseryman's convention discussing the problem with Mrs. James I. George, the well-known clematis grower.

"Name it 'Cloud 9,'" Mrs. George suggested. Henry liked the idea and introduced it as 'Cloud 9' dogwood — still the best of all the dogwood cultivars. Needless to say, whenever I see a 'Cloud 9' dogwood, I think of Henry and Mrs. George and that hotel room in Philadelphia.

Hoskins Shadow, another well-known nurseryman, always comes to mind when I see a red dogwood because he found and introduced Cherokee Chief, the best of all the deep-colored cultivars. Conversation with Hoskins when I visited his nursery never failed to turn to the heavy bloom, clean growth, and beautiful color of Hoskins' Cherokee Chief dogwood.

Of all the nurserymen I knew, Hubert Nicholson had the greatest range of knowledge. Whenever I visited Hubert in Tennessee, I added an extra day or two to my schedule so as to have plenty of time to see his new plants and the new techniques he used to propagate and grow them. His studious approach and detailed explanations were like going back to school.

Hubert decided to set aside a part of his nursery to grow large specimens of slow-growing trees like lace-leafed Japanese maple, white birch, and white spruce. He was particularly interested in European white birch and European white spruce, which were more adapted to our heat than Northern clump birch or Colorado Blue Spruce.

When the manager of one of the most prestigious clubs in Atlanta inquired one Christmas about a matched pair of white spruce for the club's Christmas decorations, I immediately thought of Hubert's specimen plantings. After several calls to Hubert and the club manager, I made the deal for two large balled-and-burlapped trees at a price so high I almost felt guilty. Hubert chose a matched pair that stood over six feet above the ground, with an estimated weight (including the ball) of more than two hundred fifty pounds. I told the manager, who agreed to the size and weight.

When our warehouse manager called me to report that the truck with the plants had arrived at our warehouse loading dock, I rushed to the window and saw two of the most beautiful white spruce trees I had ever seen. Suddenly, a worker climbed on the truck and began to saw off each tree. I was so upset I ran down three flights of stairs, quicker than ever before or since. I screamed at the poor worker, who now had both trees cut off, and at our warehouse manager who had provided the saw. Well, it turned out that our people were simply following the club manager's instructions; he wanted the trees cut, even at that exorbitant price. But I was still livid. The thought of killing those beautiful trees, especially after watching Hubert nurture them for so many years, was more than I could bear. Dad said, "Forget it. What's done is done." I tried to put it out of my mind, but I never told Hubert what happened.

Betsy and I have been to Mountain Brook, a suburb of Birmingham, Alabama, many times to visit our friends Jimmy and Jeanette Hancock who are avid gardeners and plantsmen. We visited them one spring when Mountain Brook's Yoshino cherries were at the peak of bloom. I had long been familiar with the Yoshino cherries associated with the Tidal Basin in Washington, but being a dogwood lover, I never considered them one of our beautiful

Southern flowering trees. But that springtime visit to Mountain Brook changed my mind totally. Now, I maintain that the Yoshino cherry is a far better flowering tree than the overused Bradford pear, and whenever I see one I think of Mountain Brook, Alabama, and our friends the Hancocks.

Sometimes it takes many years for a plant to become your friend. During my nursery days, Jacques Legendre, the famous horticulturist and nurseryman, sent new plants he discovered for me to try at Sweet Apple. Jacques was a commercial producer who believed plants should be grown for years before they could be properly evaluated. I planted most of his plants in a special area we affectionately called our arboretum. My attention became focused on vegetables after we sold the company, so these plants grew and grew while we lived in Egypt and Malaysia. Once back home, Chris became interested in the *Hydrangea paniculata* '*Grandiflora*' Jacques had sent me. We both realized its upright growth and huge white flowers made this an outstanding cultivar. We also pruned, fertilized, and cleaned up several other Legendre plants, several of whose names I had forgotten. One day, I smelled something delightful as I walked through the garden. My nose led me to the arboretum and a plant that turned out to be a *Clethra alnifolia*. I am glad it was left alone to grow naturally because its large size makes it inappropriate for small gardens, but excellent in the background or near woodlands. There are new dwarf cultivars that are wonderful additions to any size garden, but my large one serves as a permanent reminder of my long association with Jacques.

~

Pass-Along Plants

The wonderful tradition of pass-along plants is another example of the connection between people that adds so much to the pleasure of gardening. Momma loved it when visitors admired one of her plants enough to ask about its origins. She would cut a sprig of a special begonia or impatiens, wrap the stem in a wet paper towel, carefully cover it with foil, and graciously present it when the guest departed. It was her way of expressing thanks to the person who gave the original plants to her.

She delighted in taking visitors around her garden while describing how and where she got many different plants. One of her favorites was a huge cane-type begonia that she grew on the terrace in the summer and kept safely in her greenhouse during the winter. Momma called it her "delicosa" begonia, which I assumed was the correct name since she got it as a pass-along plant from Brother Paul, who tended the greenhouses at the Trappist Monastery outside Atlanta and who, in addition to being a begonia lover, was a noted herb and bonsai grower. Momma loved to visit Brother Paul to discuss plants and how to grow them. When she admired his "delicosa," he generously snipped off a cutting and gave it to her. She felt an obligation to pass along her good fortune by being just as generous with cuttings for visitors.

Momma gave Betsy and me a small rooted offspring of her "delicosa" when we moved to Sweet Apple many years ago. The small plant grew large and still takes its place on our screen porch each summer. I have maintained the pass-along tradition by giving cuttings to many people over the years. I gave one to our friends Frank and Jerrie Miller when they moved into their first home. The Millers have passed along cuttings just like Betsy and I have until Momma's "delicosa" is scattered all over.

When I was writing my first books, I mentioned this story, still assuming the name was correct. But when Chris and I started *Month-By-Month Gardening in the South*, he said, "Dad, I don't think Weezie (as all Momma's grandchildren called her) had that name right." We researched it and found the correct name to be *Begonia "delicosa,"* not "delicosa." I like *Begonia "deliciosa"* better since it sounds like "delicious," which fits

Momma's plant perfectly, but many of our friends still call it "delicosa" like Momma did. "Small matter," as they say in the Philippines. Regardless of the pronunciation, the pass-along *Begonia deliciosa* that started at the Monastery of the Holy Ghost near Conyers, Georgia, now graces the homes of dozens of friends and friends of friends.

Momma was determined to bring home an unusual plant from wherever she went — even from foreign countries. She and a group of ladies visited a villa in Italy with a magnificent patterned garden where she spotted an unfamiliar edging plant. It was trimmed like a box hedge but its fruit looked like an orange pepper. While the other ladies listened to the tour guide, Momma looked for the head gardener. He didn't speak English and she didn't speak Italian, but that didn't stop Momma from finding out what it was and how to grow it. At the end of the conversation — such as it was — the gardener broke off a bouquet of peppers and handed it to her. She thanked him profusely and rejoined the group.

But she had a big problem. How could she bring her beautiful pepper pods through customs? Momma was always determined and resourceful. When she dressed for the long flight home, she carefully wove her pepper bouquet into the spray of silk flowers on her trim hat and walked right past the customs inspectors. She grew those peppers for years afterward, just like she saw them in

Italy, and plucked many a bouquet of pods for people who wanted to try them in their garden.

In a similar vein, I saw a dwarf caladium growing in a small tin can on the window shelf of a house in the Philippines. It was identical to our favorite cultivar 'Candidum' but had miniature leaves. The lady of the house wanted to give the plant to me, but it seemed so rare I refused her offer. When I asked my friend Bal Balesteros where the lady might have found such a wonderful plant, he took me to a whole colony of them growing in a nearby forest. It occurred to me that a miniature caladium 'Candidum' would be wonderful in pots back home, but I confess that I wasn't nearly as bold or resourceful as my mother. I presume that they are still unknown except in that small area of the Philippines.

There are a few gardeners in the world who jealously guard their unusual or rare plants, refusing to pass them along under any condition. There are also those who will resort to any means to lay their hands on a clipping. When African violets were first becoming popular, the company decided to host an African violet show at the City Auditorium. Our manager reported several instances of women "accidentally" knocking leaves off these plants with their purses, then picking them up and making off with them.

~

Tropicals

Working abroad opened my eyes to a new world of plants. In Egypt, for example, I was fascinated to see what had become of some of our common houseplants. I saw huge rubber plants, *Ficus decora*, grown as street trees and our weeping fig, *Ficus benjamina*, frequently used as hedges. And at the Marriott Hotel in Cairo, which was constructed around a palace built when the Suez Canal was opened in 1869, the gardens were filled with enormous *Ficus benjamina* grown as shade trees.

However, none of this prepared me for the fantastic world of plant material which lay all around me in the Philippines. On my first trip, I toured the archipelago by car, helicopter, and boat looking for suitable farmland for a vegetable project. I started in the north at Baguio, which was the final stop of thousands of American and Filipino prisoners who were herded north by the Japanese in what became known as the Bataan Death March.

In stark contrast to the awful memories of the Death March shared with me by the son of a Filipino survivor was the beautiful plant material beside the road up the mountain to Baguio. Sunflowers were everywhere, turning their faces to the moving sun. These were not the huge sunflowers we like to grow but a species of helianthus with three- to four-inch-wide orange-yellow flowers. But the most interesting plants alongside the road were the many alocasias. At the time, alocasias were not widely grown in the United States, though they were common enough else-where. They are somewhat like our Elephant Ear, *Colocasia esculentum*, but much more interesting since their leaves have varied shapes and many variations of light and dark green. Tropical ferns flourished wherever they could find a bit of moisture and some shade.

Next we toured the Batangas Province south of Manila. This time we flew in by helicopter — the expe-rience of a lifetime. When the pilot put down on the large, prosperous farm we were to visit, chickens squawked, cows fled, and children came running at the strange whir of the machine. The pilot shut down the engine, and we crawled out and calmly strolled to the beautiful house like we were walking across a suburban lawn. The owner of the hacienda welcomed us into a lovely garden that featured a beautiful vine-covered arbor with hanging fruit.

As we sipped the delicious drink he offered and dis-cussed suitable land in the area, I learned that the vine was a *Passiflora*, known to us as passionfruit, and our drinks were freshly squeezed from the ripe fruits. I hadn't recognized the vine because it looked so different from the maypop that grows wild in the South, as well as from the beautiful passionflowers we saw at the tomb of Lazarus in the Holy Land.

My next search area was the far south island of Mindanao — a gardener's heaven filled with tropical plants. Our plane approached Davao airport over a dense canopy of lush trees — bananas, as it turned out. I stayed for several days at one of these banana plantations, owned by Marsman Estates Plantations, Inc., and I have never seen such a place. Not only was it a fantastic banana operation, but it was also a picture of what a profitable business can do for its workers. It had the best hospital in the area, excellent schools, fine housing, churches, and cooperative stores. But importantly to me, management encouraged recreation, especially sports and gardening. I had never seen so many orchids growing in a single place — of every kind and at almost every house.

While I was on Mindanao, I also visited Philippine Packing Company, one of the world's largest pineapple plantations, and marveled at how these wonderful fruits are grown. I could never have dreamed of seeing over ten thousand acres of pineapples in one spot. I also stopped at a field of innocuous-looking plants that turned out to be used for producing the fiber for making the beautiful and extremely cool Barang Tagalog shirts so many Filipinos wear.

Our last search area was Guimaras Island in the center of the Philippines between the large islands of Negros and Panay. Marsman had started a new mango plantation there and was interested in adding a vegetable farm alongside their current facility. It was on this island that I spent almost a year operating a test project to determine the feasibility of a large vegetable plantation project in a tropical region. Barrio Nazareth was where I found the dwarf caladiums, as well as some remarkable mature plants like frangipani, mahogany, highly fragrant Asiatic jasmine (the national favorite of Filipinos), as well as many new plants I had never seen before.

Guimaras remains one of my favorite places even though the political climate was not suitable for a full-blown project. Our crops were fantastic and the workers were wonderful. My July 4th celebration party — featuring barbecued kid, barbecued dog, and plenty of beer — was one of the most fun events of my life. One night Bal Balesteros pointed out the Southern Cross constellation, which I hadn't seen before since I had never been in the tropical zone. The huge cross of stars was spectacular, like a beacon guiding the people through those tough postrevolution times. I have seen the Southern Cross many times in Malaysia, but it was different in the Philippines because it seemed to offer hope as it hung over the wonderfully kind Filipinos of Guimaras like a shepherd leading its flock in face of the communist terror which surrounded us all the time.

Singapore, too, was filled with plants I had never seen before, like the beautiful Sealing Wax Palm, which is widely grown in pots inside buildings as well as outside in gardens. The trunks are a brilliant red, distinguishing them from any other palm I have ever seen. I have no idea why these striking plants have never been widely used in the United States.

In Malaysia, Betsy became the gardener since I was busy from sunup to sunset trying to solve insect, disease, and growth problems on our vegetables. She inherited huge pots of feebly growing Bougainvillea across the front of our house in Kuala Lumpur. Within a short time, she brought them to life with regular water and fertilizer. From then on, they never stopped blooming. Our yard was filled with things new to me — like crab's claws, *Helconia rostrata;* flowering ginger, *Zingiber officinalis;* the lovely MacArthur palm, which attracted a brilliant yellow-colored bird; rambutan, a delightful fruit; and several mangoes whose fruit wasn't so good but which served as excellent places for Betsy to hang her orchid collection.

One night when I arrived home, Betsy wanted to show me some new orchids she had found. They were really beautiful, especially the delicate Dancing Lady, which is a favorite in Malaysia and Singapore.

"Where did you get such beautiful plants?" I asked.

She mumbled around about going to some nursery area on the edge of town. I wanted to go see the place and pressed her further.

"It's at the leper colony," she finally told me. The ancient fear of leprosy awakened in me, but I kept my feelings to myself. The next day I asked my sales manager, Alex Chan, about the best place to find good orchid plants.

"At the leper colony," he replied enthusiastically. "Do you want me to take you?"

I drew up some courage, said yes, and off we went. We passed through the hospital grounds and came to a number of small nurseries filled with an incredible variety of tropical plants. When we finally arrived at the orchid section, I was astonished at the vast array of these beautiful flowers, many of which were unique crosses by the owner. Some of the most spectacular sold for hundreds of dollars each, and cars with tags from all over Malaysia brought orchid lovers to this unusual spot.

By the way, Alex told me that many of the workers in the nurseries were, in fact, infected with leprosy, but that modern science and treatment kept the once-dreaded disease under control. This information almost made me feel better about Betsy having visited the place without telling me beforehand.

~

Back Home

I was walking along the Corniche in Alexandria, Egypt, one night, waiting for a telex to come from the U.S.A., when I was approached by a friendly group of university students. Before long we were immersed in a deep discussion of all sorts of human and political subjects. One boy asked, after I told him how much I liked Alexandria, "Which is best, Alexandria or your city in Amerikki?"

"Alexandria is a wonderful city," I replied, using all of my mental dexterity, "and I like it very much, but home is always the best place. When you come to Atlanta, I hope you will like it a lot, but I won't be mad when you say that Alexandria is better. I will know how you feel." They smiled and offered to buy me tea so I could tell them more about my home city.

I would not give anything for my fascinating first-hand introduction to tropical plants while I was in Egypt and in Southeast Asia. But I will always like the plants of the southeastern United States better. They are "home plants" — mine to love and enjoy — and I won't be mad if Egyptian, Filipino, or Malaysian friends say their "home plants" are better.

The only exception to my devotion to my "home

plants" is weeds. I concede that weeds show the marvelous diversity of the plant kingdom, and I understand the point of Charles Hudson's expression, "A weed is any plant out of place." But knowing the names of weeds and their proper identification has never interested me very much. I find myself returning to the weed manuals over and over for the name of a weed I have seen many times; I can't remember their names. And it's no wonder. "Cutting weeds" was my introduction into the nursery business, and that backbreaking work under the hot sun when I was thirteen remains too real for me to look on weeds as anything but nameless, faceless pests. If you ask me, "What's that weed?" my answer is to get out the Weed-Eater and say, "What weed?"

Of course, this prejudice does not extend to all wild-growing plants. To me, Queen Anne's lace, butterfly weed, Joe-Pye weed, and maypop — just to name a few — are beautiful enough to cultivate in my garden, and natural areas are transformed by their presence. But that doesn't mean there's any excuse for nutgrass, stinging nettle, crabgrass, chickweed, and kudzu — plants which clearly have no redeeming value.

The modern fad of having "natural" gardens to "live within the environment" is nonsense. There is no *paradeisos* in the weed patch. Quite the opposite — to me weeds represent that unpleasant place we live good lives to avoid.

Part Two

Chapter Four

The Garden Today

Liberty Hyde Bailey often reminisced about changes during his lifetime. He was born when Indians were a threat to life and property in his part of Michigan, yet he lived long enough to see the beginning of the technology explosion that has changed all our lives. Since those days when we students listened to Dr. Bailey, plant scientists have made extraordinary progress, like identifying DNA and using genetic engineering, which have led to a better understanding of all plant processes.

But in spite of all the progress of the last one hundred years, plants still grow the same as they always have, and people often make a mess of things as they always have. It's true that fertilizers are more potent, pesticides are more effective, and power tools help us keep gardens looking neat with a lot less effort, and it is said that interest in gardening today is greater than ever before. But I

believe it is ever more difficult to develop an understanding of how to grow plants because most of us grow
up in a city rather than on farms.

I noticed this change during my years as a garden talk
show host. In the early years, a great many of my callers
had farm backgrounds, along with a birth-to-grave
dependency on growing plants successfully or suffering
the consequences. On the farm, a whim of nature might
destroy a rural family's chances for enough food to survive; nowadays a late frost requires urban gardeners to
simply set out a few new tomato plants.

Rosa Weems, one of my regular callers, was born on a
farm in Central Georgia. She always called early when
most city folks were still asleep and when I had to fill the
air with stuff from my own brain. "I figured you needed
someone to prime the pump," Rosa would gently say,
referring to a hand-operated well-pump which was readied by pouring water into the system. Rosa and I became
good friends as we talked about rural life on Saturday
mornings. She remembered white sweet potatoes, cutting
okra, priming pumps, picking cotton (which we both
hated), and hog killing on a frosty November day.

Gradually my audience changed until I had only a few
who could remember going to grandpa's farm, much less
identify guano or a scooter plow. The new gardeners
wanted specific instructions from me like those found in

the operator's manual of a car or home appliance. Rosa understood this as well as I did, and we talked about farming in such a way as to help listeners come to a broader understanding of plants and their needs.

I well remember the devastating consequences of the Great Depression; yet somehow people survived because of a deep faith in their own ability to grow enough food. Many years later in the Philippines, I found the same sort of will to survive among those who had endured the Marcos dictatorship. Though the average income was only one or two hundred dollars per year in the rural areas, the people kept themselves well fed by growing much of their own food and sending their children to fish in the sea or dive for crabs and lobsters near the shore. Most families grew rice for their own consumption and enough extra to sell for other necessities. Every boy learned to shinny up a coconut tree where he could find plentiful supplies of the nutritious fruit.

Now I don't have to grow my own food, but I want to. We all have a primordial instinct to grow things, to be productive. Furnishing our own table — whether with fresh vegetables or with fresh-cut flowers — is deeply satisfying. Today, for the most part, we buy everything and individually produce nothing, not even our own fun. A young nurseryman quoted the modern attitude: "Here's a dollar. Make me happy." Nevertheless, there remains a need in our lives to produce something from our own land. A place of peace and quiet is as important now as ever before.

I like to visit a nursery in the spring because the frantic buying of plants and supplies takes me back to my many years as a nurseryman. Spring in a nursery is like Christmas in a mall, and the expectancy on the faces of adults and children alike is a sight to see. At the same time, my years in the business sound an alarm when I see so many different kinds of plants being loaded into waiting cars. How many will live and how many will die? Will these gardeners end up rejoicing, or will they want to pave over the yard? New plants stream out of a nursery in March and April. Failures stream back in May and June.

One extremely busy Sunday at our nursery, a line of people were waiting to ask me questions when a rather belligerent man strode to the head of the line and thrust a handful of dead roses and a slip of paper at me.

"These plants are no good," he bellowed. "Look, they all died and I planted them exactly according to your instructions. I want my money back."

They were the strangest looking dead plants I had ever seen. Every cane was brown except for an inch of green at the top. I was determined to find out what had happened, but the man would only shout, "I planted them according to the directions." Finally I walked over, found replacements, and held them out. But when he started to grab the plants, I held on.

"I am going to give you these as replacements but first you must tell me exactly how you planted these dead ones."

"Exactly like that says," he replied, poking the instruction slip.

"I understand that, but I know they were planted wrong, and I want to rewrite the instructions if they confused you," I gently said.

Finally he told me he dug a hole eighteen inches deep and twenty-four inches wide, then made the cone in the bottom of the hole, placed the roots over it, and packed prepared soil around the plant, "Just like it said to do," he repeated once again.

Suddenly I realized what he had done. "Show me where the soil covered the stems," I asked. When he pointed to the line where the green started, I showed him the instructions about placing the graft union on top of the soil when planting. He grabbed the replacements and hurried out.

I could not understand how he thought a plant so deeply buried would grow, until I realized that the man had probably never planted anything in his life. He had no background for understanding the functions of the roots, stems, and branches of a plant, nor for understanding the instructions. Rosa would say, "You can lead a horse to water but you can't make it drink."

I visited the Royal Botanical Gardens at Kew near London (most often referred to as Kew Gardens), fulfilling a desire dating back to my college days. British explorers have been searching the world for plants to bring back to England since before the United States became a nation. Kew Gardens, which developed on the grounds of King George III's palace, is the repository for many of them. The plantings at Kew evolved into the Royal Botanical Garden, now a haven for plant lovers from around the world.

I went to see famous mature trees like giant redwoods from our country, cryptomeria from Japan, and others from many parts of the world. But what I found fascinating were the glass houses designed to replicate specific climatic conditions — temperate, tropical, Alpine houses, and so on. My first day at Kew was cold and rainy so I darted into the Evolution House to warm up and dry out. Inside was a recreation of the conditions under which our Creator began life on earth. At the entrance was a bubbling mud cauldron surrounded by primitive plant organisms, and from there the path led from one area to the next, each representing a new evolutionary phase in plant development. The self-guided tour ended with well-formed ferns and mosses.

The other glass houses opened my eyes to the marvels of plant acclimation and adaption. I realized more than ever before how important the total environment of a garden is, not just how hot or cold it gets or how much rain falls. Soils in parts of the United States and England have a very high pH, while others, like most of the South, have a much lower pH. Azaleas and hollies need low pH while peonies and lilacs need it high, and woe be to the gardener who doesn't amend the soil to suit the plants he is growing.

Milton Nardin, the manager of our Cheshire Bridge Road nursery before I left the company, sold a number of Savannah hollies to a lady whose home was on his route to work. After they were planted, he noticed her yard man applying lime around them. Milton stopped and found the lady and politely urged her to stop the application. She not only refused to interfere, but told Milton it was none of his business what the yardman did.

"Okay," Milton said, "but remember — I asked you not to put lime on these hollies and when they die, I will not replace them."

"They will not die," she responded.

As he drove to work each day, Milton watched the plants begin to turn yellow. Before the season was over, they were dead. Of course the lady came back for replacements, and Milton refused, reminding her of his warning. She went up the chain of command through me to Dad, but since Milton had told Dad and me the story, we also refused to accommodate her — which made her absolutely furious. I'm happy to report that after she realized her error, the lady apologized to us all and subsequently became one of the nicest customers we had. But the story illustrates some fundamental truths.

Like it always has, success in gardening today comes from a feeling for plants and then an understanding of their needs within the micro-environment you've placed them in. Start with good soil, carefully select which plants to grow, plant them right, and look after them by fertilizing, pruning, and controlling pests.

I don't have any idea why some people grow plants successfully while others who work as hard are unsuccessful. Dad was a Presbyterian and thought it took hard work to make a plant grow well. Momma was an Episcopalian who saw a miracle when a tiny seed developed into a plant with a beautiful flower. I believe you must *want* a plant in your garden in order for it to grow; that desire might well lead to developing the expertise that every gardener needs. Beyond that, I readily confess that there is much I don't know, which makes me more an Episcopalian than a Presbyterian. When I dig a big hole, mix the soil right, and plant something which produces beauty in my garden, I see a miracle even though my back may hurt.

Chapter Five

Planting

The sower went out to sow his seed; and as he sowed,
some fell beside the road; and it was trampled under
foot, and the birds of the air ate it up.
And other seed fell on rocky soil, and as soon as it
grew up, it withered away, because it had no moisture.
And other seed fell among the thorns; and the thorns
grew up with it, and choked it out.
And other seed fell into the good soil, and grew up,
and produced a crop a hundred times as great.

— Luke 8:5–8
NASB

I was born with a garden trowel in my hand instead of
a silver spoon in my mouth. When I was old enough to
be in the garden, I watched Willie plant Momma's flowers and asked four-year-old boy questions like, "Whatcha

doing? What's that? Why you doing it that way?" Willie was as patient as Job, understanding from his own children that my questions were a child's way of conversing and that his answers didn't really matter. Sure enough, I would soon get bored with what Willie was doing and wander away to watch the fish in the garden pool . . . and maybe fall in.

Momma and Dad talked a lot about planting. Dad focused on the next season's crops while Momma looked further into the future, "I want a background with camellias and rhododendrons between the house and the pool garden. They will be just right when you are grown and have a wife and children," she would tell me. She believed that land should belong to many generations, not just one.

I watched intently when the farm crew brought huge Lawson cypress and dug big holes to plant them in. I liked watching the hard work as they dragged each big plant and carefully wrestled it into its hole. Momma explained why they dug the holes so big and why they mixed stuff in the soil that they packed around the balls after they set the plants in the holes. I must have thought at the time that Momma was telling me more than I wanted to know, but I suppose she was nurturing me just like she nurtured her garden.

Just about anything Momma put in the ground flourished. The one exception was asparagus. The year she had the big Lawson cypress put in, she also planted her first asparagus bed. The men from the farm came over to help, bringing with them a load of stable manure, which Momma had heard made asparagus grow well. Willie had laid a low rock wall around the bedding area, and we watched the men fill the bed with a layer of soil from the field and a layer of manure and then mix the two together. The bed was finished . . . except for the planting. Momma and Willie did that. The plants started growing but never really took off, and none came back the next year. She tried for two more years . . . no asparagus.

One Sunday Momma and I were riding our horses around the terraces in the field in front of the house.

"Look here," I heard her call. "Look at all this asparagus!"

I turned Lady and rode back beside her, and, sure enough, there was a huge colony of asparagus growing on the ditch bank. We found more colonies on ditch banks in other parts of the field, and still more on ditch banks in other fields. The farm was full of naturally growing asparagus.

Momma never tried again; she had learned her lesson: "The Lord knows where to plant asparagus, and I don't," she said. But cutting asparagus on the ditch banks became a regular part of our Sunday rides.

I didn't do much planting when I worked on the farm since most of that work was finished by the time I got out of school. Small shrubs and trees were set out in the winter to be ready to grow when the weather warmed. Magnolia and dogwood seeds were planted in the fall and again in the spring. The farm crew planted Hastings Prolific Corn as soon as the danger of frost was over in April, then watermelons, okra, and cotton when the ground warmed in early May. By the time school was out and I was getting up at 5:00 a.m. to work in the fields for the summer, everything was up and growing. Dad's trial grounds were at a stage where he could make his weekly observations and enter his opinions in the records. Oats and wheat had been planted the previous fall and were deep green and ready to send up the stalks on which the grain would form.

I began to develop a deep interest in planting after I came home from Cornell and began working in our seed and nursery business in Atlanta. But I learned the most about planting when Betsy and I moved to Sweet Apple, north of the city beyond Roswell. We wanted shrubs, trees, fruits, flowers, and vegetables on our twenty acres. Finally I had my own place to grow all the types of plants I liked or wanted to try. Success there depended on my mind and my back, not on the theories or experiences of others. Sweet Apple became my earthly *paradeisos*.

Later, in our commercial projects overseas, we planted large acreages of vegetables like tomatoes, okra, lettuce, and broccoli instead of the few twenty-foot rows I planted in my Sweet Apple garden. When something did poorly for me at Sweet Apple, I learned from my mistakes and replanted, but when seeds didn't come up in a hundred-acre field, the project's program was seriously hurt. Productive fields started with good planting techniques. Growth-related problems, like proper irrigating, fertilizing, and controlling insects and diseases, came after seeds germinated and started to grow. The first step — planting — was the critical one. When Dad said to start every gardening project on your knees, he was referring to good soil preparation, but of course soil preparation is simply the beginning of success with any plant.

When our nursery customers would bring back dead or dying plants, the vast majority had been planted without preparing the soil well. It was sad to look at them: their roots had never had a chance to grow and support their tops. Too often they were covered with hard clods of clay. Few people seemed to follow our planting instructions. Few people seemed willing to do the work.

Plants — except for weeds — don't just grow in a garden. They have to be planted correctly, then nurtured carefully in order to live up to expectations. You also have to choose the right plant for any given situation. Water lilies won't grow in the desert nor cacti in a jungle. A good gardener learns to be a good doctor by diagnosing growth problems and reacting to them. But gardening always begins on your knees.

Soon after I went to work in the company, I had a lesson on what some homeowners mean when they talk about planting. A customer complained to me that his lawn was in bad shape and asked how to improve it.

"I want a beautiful green lawn all year. Tell me the best grass and how to plant it," he said emphatically.

I told him to plant Kentucky 31 fescue in the sunny parts and to mix it half-and-half with Creeping Red fescue for the shadier areas.

"What do I have to do before I sow the seed?" he asked.

I told him to till the area thoroughly, work in peat moss, lime, and fertilizer, rake it until smooth, then sow six to eight pounds of seed per thousand square feet. This was my first "prescription" after graduation, and I wrote down the amounts of each item needed for a thousand square feet. "Measure your lawn and figure how much of each you will need," I told him proudly.

He looked at the slip of paper, then said adamantly, "That's too much work. Figure how much rye grass I will need and get it for me."

I was undone. "But it will die when it gets hot," I sputtered.

"I don't care. It will be green from now until then," he replied.

I lowered my standards and sold him rye grass and some cheap fertilizer.

When the man left, I asked Vic Moore, one of our lawn experts, if people always thought that way. "Don't let it bother you," Vic said with a laugh. "He'll be back next spring for some other kind of seed to take him through the summer."

Of course there are exceptions to every gardening rule, even one as fundamental as "planting takes work."

Whenever the farm truck drove into the nursery, I would look for Coot and Wilbert. Like most intelligent country people, they had a wonderful way of talking to each other about things that somebody else — like me — might like to hear or need to know.

One afternoon I saw them drive in with a truck full of balled-and-burlapped plants for the nursery, along with some mail-order-size azaleas. The packing house had closed so I asked where they were taking the azaleas.

"They're for Ma Hastings. She bought all the left-overs," Coot replied. They were nice plants, but I had no idea where Momma was going to plant them.

"Coot, you ever see Miss Louise plant stuff like this?" Wilbert asked.

"Ain't it something. I never saw anybody plant like she does," Coot replied.

I knew Wilbert wanted to tell me how Momma planted, so I chimed in, "How does she plant?"

"She takes her toe, scrootches out a little hole in the woods, drops one in, then stomps on it. That's all," was Wilbert's reply.

"And they all live," Coot added.

"Sure do. Don't see how, but they sure do," Wilbert said and sighed.

Wilbert's own method was a far cry from Momma's scrootching out a hole with her toe and stomping on the ball. He was an artist, and the best planter we had in the company. He carefully measured the ball, then dug the hole larger and deeper. He mixed peat moss with the soil he took from the hole like he was mixing dough for bread. He refilled the hole just enough so the top of the ball wouldn't need covering. Then he shoveled mixed soil around the ball and packed it tight with the shovel handle. Finally he made a dam around the plant and slowly soaked it with a hose. As painstaking as he was, he was also so efficient that he finished the whole job before the other planters dug their holes and mixed their soil.

His plants always lived, too. If you have the magic touch like Momma did, maybe you can get away with the toescrootch, no-work planting method. But for everybody else, I'd recommend Wilbert's. It's work, but it works.

≈

Seeds

My grandfather started his company in 1889 to sell seeds, but by the time we opened our first garden center in the early fifties, the emphasis was on plants. We still carried a full range of flower, vegetable, and lawn grass seeds under the Hastings Seeds brand, and until we sold the company most people still called it Hastings Seed Company. I considered myself both a seedsman and a nurseryman because I liked to grow plants from seeds as much as growing plants which someone else started.

One of my sideline hobbies is collecting seeds from plants I discover in strange and wonderful places, like some vitex seeds I spotted at a rest stop on I-16 to Savannah, Georgia. Some collected seeds won't germinate, but those that do always have special meaning. One of my best finds was from a group of dawn redwood trees in front of Walk Thru the Bible Ministries in Atlanta where Betsy works. She gathered several cones for me from which I extracted and planted the seeds. I now have three perfectly beautiful dawn redwoods.

But being a seed collector can also cause problems. After my first success with Betsy's dawn redwood seed, I stopped by one afternoon to see her and noticed the cones were just right for seed-harvesting. So I started plucking them off the branches, without a single thought as to how funny I looked picking at the trees in front of a well-respected business. When Betsy came home that night, she told me that the receptionist had been ready to call a padded wagon. Betsy had had to explain to her that I wasn't really a nut, but a seed collector — a close relative perhaps.

I also have to be careful with the seeds I collect, put in my pocket, and forget about. One day when Betsy was washing my shirts she found something in a pocket which she thought was an M&M candy. When I got home she was laughing. "I was really mad when I thought you bought a bag of M&M's and didn't share them, so I decided to get even and popped the one you left in your pocket in my mouth. It was awful. What on earth was it?"

I thought and thought, then realized it was a *Camellia sasanqua* seed I had found.

I think planting seeds is as important a skill to master as planting already growing trees, shrubs, fruits, flowers, or vegetables. When I start my plants from seeds, I have exactly the vegetables or flowers I want. It irritates me when I go to a nursery and can't find the cultivars I want or, worse yet, find a tray with no label or one with mixed plants. I want what I want, not something else that might mess up my plantings. My vegetable garden is my pride and joy and I want specific types and cultivars, not some generic or unidentified plants. I have always been like that, but since growing vegetables overseas I am even more particular.

In Egypt, we grew over five hundred acres of tomatoes for the European market — the most exacting market I have ever shipped to. We had to sell our tomatoes by size. If a buyer ordered small "salad" tomatoes (35- to 50-mm) and we shipped "beef" (100- to 108-mm) tomatoes, he refused the shipment. We not only lost the cost of growing and packing but the tremendous cost of air transport to the market. In Europe, bigger is not always better, so we chose our tomato cultivars carefully to fit the requirements.

In Asia, growing the right cultivars was also important. Malaysian customers demanded a five-angled (ridged) okra while Singapore's market required okra with seven angles. Singaporians would buy only yellow sweet corn while Hong Kong paid a premium for the bicolor cultivars. Seed purity, as well as having the right cultivars, is extremely important and determines the price you get on a given market. To a project like ours, a good price is the difference between success and failure.

I start my flower seeds in seed trays with cells because the seeds are small. If I seeded them directly in the garden, heavy spring rains would either wash them away or bury them too deeply. Of course, Nature does the job right; many of my established perennials reseed themselves in the flower bed, and Marguerite daisy, butterfly weed, and maypop come up in my pasture with no help from me. There must be a lesson there, but I don't seem to have passed the exam yet.

I directly seed vegetables that have large seeds — corn, squash, melons, and cucumbers — but start small-seeded types like tomato, pepper, and eggplant in seed trays at the same time I plant summer flower seed in trays. Of course, planting seeds and then waiting for them to germinate will test a gardener's patience. Every day I walk through my greenhouse or garden searching for the first leaves piercing the surface and reaching upward toward the sun. A week of waiting seems a lifetime and two weeks are deadly to my psyche. Malaysia was better for my nerves since germination is quicker in the warm soil. Waiting was still awful, but on the third or fourth day I knew we had taken the first step toward a good crop when I saw unbroken lines of green seedlings stretching across a field.

The success or failure of a crop is often determined by the depth seeds are planted. The heavy clay soil at Sweet Apple develops a crust when hot sun follows a rain. Small seeds have a tough time breaking through it. Sometimes they run out of gas, so to speak, before they get out of the ground, especially when the soil hasn't been prepared well.

In our projects overseas, depth of planting was even more critical. If planted too deeply, supersweet corn and okra fail to germinate well because they have too little starch to push through to the surface. I once watched a field of newly-planted supersweet corn with great anticipation because the market price in Hong Kong was heading higher. When the corn began to germinate, I saw to my horror that the field had terrible skips in it. I walked back and forth through the rows trying to discover the cause of the problem. Nongermination had occurred in a strange but regular pattern. I couldn't figure it out, and Chet, our field manager, was as stumped as I.

"It's the pots," Chet said suddenly. The "pots" were the individual seed planter units which ride on a bar behind a tractor. Chet found the planter in another field and discovered that a bolt holding one side of the pot had broken, causing it to place the seeds deeper than we wanted. Every sixth row was almost empty while all the rest had excellent germination. When such disasters occurred, we often plowed up a field and started over, but in this case, five-sixths of a crop was worthwhile since we would hit the market exactly right.

With the sweet corn in my garden, I'm not so concerned about market timing, but timing is still important; it determines how many worms will attack. Early planting means early harvesting and fewer worm problems. Late plantings are a mess because ears are silking when worm populations are reaching their peak. At Sweet Apple north of Atlanta, I try to plant sweet corn the first week of May each year.

Ferns are plants I've always wanted to grow from seed — or spores, in this case — but I've never been too successful. Momma had a beautiful climbing fern growing on an arch between two of her gardens, and underneath were many "seedlings" which she would dig and give to friends who admired its beauty. One day I noticed spores on the leaves of the parent, so I plucked some and took them to Sweet Apple. Not a one germinated, so I did what everybody else did — dug a seedling to start in my greenhouse. It grew well and continues to come back each year.

One hot summer day I was visiting Overlook Nurseries near Mobile, Alabama, which was started by the famous plantsman and grower, Kay Sawada. His son

Tom became a good friend as well as one of our best suppliers. Walking through the nursery I saw some beautiful lace-leaf ferns climbing on stakes placed in the pots. I thought I recognized the plant from the huge one in Momma's garden. Momma called it a Climbing Maidenhair fern.

"What's this?" I asked Tom, pointing to the row of plants.

"I just call it climbing fern," he replied.

I bought some, and we sold it well enough for us to need more than Tom was growing. On a visit to Glen St. Mary Nurseries in Florida, I asked Lyn Taber if he had any climbing ferns. I remembered at one time they grew many ferns from spores.

"I never heard of it," Lyn replied.

Driving around the container fields, I noticed a vine covering the irrigation standpipes and walked over to see what it was. "Lyn, here is the fern I asked about," I called out.

Lyn walked over, looked at the plant and started laughing. "What do you want that for? It's a mess. We spray to kill it."

"It sells well for us and we can't find all we need," I replied, not really believing that Lyn considered it a pest.

"Send a crew down. I'll give you all you want," Lyn replied. He obviously meant what he said.

Some gardeners are more patient than I when it comes to growing ferns from spores. I found several pots in the greenhouse in which Chris had planted a number of different ferns. I was excited to see the tiny first-stage ferns, but I am very willing to pass the spore-growing mantle to him.

For the record, the climbing fern is a *Lygodium* and has nothing to do with maidenhair ferns. I have no idea where Momma got the name Climbing Maidenhair fern but I suspect she made it up.

~

Roots

In my nursery business days, we carried a wide variety of bare-root plants: fruit trees, pecans, bush berries, grapes, smaller shade trees, and roses. Most bare-root plants that died and were returned for replacements had been planted at the incorrect depth. Ex-farmers often planted them too deeply, since they were used to setting tomato and pepper plants more deeply than they were growing and tended to apply the same principle to bare-root stock. Urban gardeners tended to plant bare-root stock too shallow, perhaps because digging a deep hole was difficult in their bulldozed topsoil. We spent — and perhaps wasted — a lot of time trying to instruct our customers to plant properly.

Pecan trees were the hardest to plant of all our bare-root stock because a three-foot tree would have a tap root over two feet long. Customers would ask, "How deep does this have to be planted?" We pointed to a spot on the trunk. "Can I use a posthole digger?" We explained it would take a larger hole than a posthole for a pecan tree to grow well. More than one person gave up growing pecan trees before ever buying one.

Nurserymen would bud-graft a cultivar on a two-year-old seedling pecan, but if the bud failed to grow, they made a regular graft to keep from losing the two-year-old seedling. The result was two places which looked like the top of the root system and the proper planting depth. This added to the difficulty.

Stuart Simpson produced our pecan trees as well as our watermelon seed in Florida. Since he was the kind of nurseryman who liked to help us solve problems, he marked his trees with paint where the soil level should be. Hubert Nicholson also used this marking method for the fruit trees which he grew for us. Once our growers started marking the planting level, our returns and complaints about failures dropped tremendously.

When I first worked in our retail nursery, container stock

was unheard of, but within a few years most smaller plants were grown this way. Not surprisingly, Coot and Wilbert developed their own unique method for planting container-grown plants. Watching them get ready to set out a line of box leaf hollies in front of a house one day, I noticed a two-by-eight board lying beside the line of holes they dug. When they removed each plant from its container, they grabbed it by the main trunk and whopped it against the two-by-eight. Roots came flying away from the ball. Then they planted it the same way as they would a balled-and-burlapped plant.

"Whatcha doing that for?" I asked in amazement.

"Gotta loosen them roots or they'll stick in the ball," Coot replied.

"I never heard of such a thing," I said. Coot shrugged and said nothing.

"Can't do it with a B&B plant, though," Wilbert added.

I have seen other nurserymen cut tightly bound roots with a knife or pull them loose with their fingers, but I have never seen any other planters whop the ball against a two-by-eight. Wilbert's and Coot's way worked fine, of course, and was much faster than laboriously cutting the roots with a knife or pulling them away from the ball with your fingers.

Wilbert used a similar method for planting sod. He

would lay out several blocks, then take the back of a flat spade and whop each one to loosen the roots and promote their growth in the freshly tilled soil underneath. I never saw one of Wilbert's sod jobs develop dead spots.

I adopted the same principle for setting out small plants grown in pots or cell packs. Our family tradition is for us boys to plant a flower garden for Betsy's Mother's Day present. I till the bed and prepare the soil, then all of us plant the small annuals she chooses. At first the rest of the family balked at my method of squeezing the small root ball rather forcefully to loosen the roots. They were sure it would damage the tiny plants, but when the plants thrived, they came around to my way of thinking. Now squeezing the root balls is a favorite part of our planting routine.

I also grow many plants in pots, especially the tropicals we came to love when we lived in Southeast Asia. They are fast growing and need repotting every year. Their roots become tightly packed around the edge of the ball and are hard to pull loose. Rather than whopping the balls against a board or cutting them with a knife, I use the method taught me by my radio and TV partner, Kathy Henderson. She uses the blunt side of her pruning shears to break apart the tightly bound roots, then pulls them loose with her fingers.

Wilbert worked at our new mail-order packing facility located on the large tract of land that also housed the Cascade Road Garden Center, our second modern garden center. After the mail-order season finished, most of the workers went back to their land to grow crops during the summer, but Coot, Wilbert, and Bennie — one of our longtime packing department employees — remained as large-order delivery men and landscapers under Raiford Broome, the Cascade Road Garden Center manager. Raiford grew up on a farm in Mississippi and had a special affinity for good farm people like Wilbert, Coot, and Bennie.

Raiford also understood plants and their growth habits, particularly how different types of plants developed their root systems. He showed me a dead two gallon-size box leaf holly that a customer brought in.

"What caused it to die?" Raiford asked. I knew that he knew, and that he was going to tell me.

"The roots never developed," I said. "You can see that they never broke from the ball."

"You can't spot-plant fibrous rooted plants like boxwood, box leaf hollies, and azaleas. You have to work a bed, then plant," he stated, answering the question that my answer raised.

Raiford theorized — and I agreed — that spot-planting shallow-growing, fibrous-rooted plants in heavy clay was dangerous even when a large hole was dug. The best way to insure success was to create a bed-like area with good depth, then work in peat moss and perlite and set the plant shallowly. Under Raiford's tutelage, we even revised our usual warranty for shallow-rooted shrubs: a one-year guarantee on bed-planted shrubs, but on spot-planted shrubs only a "begin-to-grow" warranty.

I spent as much time at the Cascade Road store as possible but not as much as I would have liked. It was very different from the northside Cheshire Bridge Road facility because of the many formerly rural people who came to shop. Raiford and I had fun translating the terms used by these customers into language familiar to the more urban members of the staff.

Raiford told me that he had a delivery near Sweet Apple, and asked if I wanted the farm crew to bring me anything. I made a list of several items, one of which was some sweet potato slips, which is what we called small sweet potato plants to set in the garden.

"You ever heard these called 'tater drawers?" Wilbert asked while unloading the truck at my house.

"No, have you?" I asked.

"Not 'til Mr. Broome told me about a lady who came in wanting some 'tater drawers." I knew Wilbert had a story to tell.

"What happened?" I asked.

"This lady asked Mr. Broome for some 'tater drawers. I don't think he knew what she was talking about so he showed her some 'tater slips. She said, 'That's them.' Mr. Broome told her they were 'tater slips. She laughed and laughed and told Mr. Broome that she guessed he was right 'cause 'taters, just like chillun, probably come from slips." We all hollered with laughter.

Wilbert asked me if I had ever planted 'tater slips. I admitted that I hadn't, so he immediately took charge in the garden. He opened several furrows, then made a large shallow hole at the end of the first row. Then he asked, "Where's the hose pipe?" I dragged the hose to the furrow and turned it on, even though I was surprised that Wilbert was watering before he planted the slips.

"Whatcha doing?" I asked as he filled the hole at the end of the row.

"I'll show you the best way to plant 'tater slips and have them live," Wilbert replied.

Bennie worked in more soil until the hole was filled with a sloppy, muddy mess.

"You need to muddy the roots since 'tater slips got so few of 'em. Keeps 'em from drying out 'til they get started," Wilbert told me. I was amazed.

Wilbert cut the bundle loose and lined them on the edge of the mud hole so the roots were covered with the muddy soup. Then he took a few at a time to plant in the furrows.

Wilbert must have learned this way of planting when he was growing up since it worked so well. I don't think I lost a single plant, and I harvested a great crop of sweet potatoes in the fall.

Many years later when Chris came back from Cornell, we talked at length about the physiological reasons for Wilbert's success muddying sweet potato slips. Chris had studied the new theories of soil interfaces, which meant very little to me, but after a long explanation accompanied by many drawings, I decided country people knew the right way to plant almost fifty years before the scientists discovered the reasons why it worked so well.

Chapter Six

Fertilizing

Early to bed, early to rise,
Work like hell, and fertilize.
    — A gardener's motto from the old days

"You boys take the truck up to the barn and get some guano," Mr. Watts directed, pronouncing the word *gu-anna*, "and meet me at the seedling chestnuts." We walked to the barn while Wilbert backed the truck up to the barn door. Then we half-carried, half-dragged the heavy bags of fertilizer out to the truck. The men lifted them onto the bed, then we rode to the Chinese chestnut field. Our job was to fill the hoppers of the mule-drawn fertilizer distributors used to side-dress the small seedlings. "Gwano" was the correct pronunciation, but to the Georgia farmers I grew up around, the term was "gu-anna."

In the minds of Georgia farmers, guano was any fertilizer coming from a fertilizer factory, like the 5-10-15 we were putting on the chestnuts. Technically, however, guano was sea bird droppings found on islands and cliffs off the western coast of South America. This rich material had weathered into an excellent fertilizer containing the three major plant nutrients — nitrogen, phosphorous, and potash. In the old days, real guano was bagged and shipped as it was gathered and without any alteration, but by my time the deposits were almost gone, and little if any of the real stuff came to Georgia. Some farmers called nitrate of soda from Chile "guano," but we called that "soda."

When we first started planting crops at our project in Malaysia, I asked Mr. Loi, our administrative manager, which organic fertilizers they used. "Everybody uses chicken dung," he replied, "but you can get others, like guano."

It took awhile for me to connect his correct Chinese/English pronunciation of "gwano" with the way Mr. Watts said "gu-anna," but I was delighted to realize that my old friend "gu-anna" had returned to my life. When Mr. Loi explained that guano was plentiful in the bat caves of the northern states, I figured out that

Malaysians use the term *guano* to refer to bat dung, rather than South American bird droppings.

But in the meantime, it was chicken dung — huge amounts of it — that Chinese farmers in Malaysia preferred to use on their crops. In our project, I found it more valuable as a source of organic matter than fertilizer nutrients because its nutrient content varied significantly from one provider to another. I also grumbled constantly about using chicken dung because of the enormous numbers of flies that came after applying it on a field. But it was like pulling eye teeth to get our managers to use anything else.

~

Rich Aromas

It was on my first trip to Malaysia and its Cameron Highlands, where Malaysia's vegetable and cut flower production is centered because the air is cool, that I was introduced to their chicken dung. A Chinese friend got in touch with me at my island project in the Philippines, insisting that I fly to Kuala Lumpur and drive with him to the highlands. The farmers were having serious problems with pesticide residues on their vegetables — so serious that Singapore, their biggest market, had condemned a large number of shipments. The farmers were desperate. I finally agreed to go with him to help find a solution to their problem.

The trip was worthwhile for me, but probably not very helpful to the Chinese farmers. I visited a number of fields, watched them spray, and checked their application rates as best I could. I spotted a possible problem. The farms are too small for power sprayers, so all chemicals were applied with hand-held backpack sprayers. At a meeting of a farmers' group I told them, "I think your problem lies in the backpack sprayers. There's no consistency in the way you apply your chemicals. One of you might pump too hard and apply too much chemical on a given plant while another might pump too easy and apply too little. I suggest you band together and buy power sprayers with regulators." In the U.S. we have contract applicators who use large machines that carefully regulate the amounts applied, and I suggested that they try something like that. It wasn't the easy answer they wanted, but I couldn't see anything else they were doing wrong.

Meanwhile, the whole time I was there the flies were as irritating as gnats on a hot summer day in Georgia. Our barns at Lovejoy on a rainy day were as sanitary as a hospital compared to what I experienced in the Cameron Highlands of Malaysia.

"Where in the name of goodness do all these flies come from?" I asked my friend.

"What flies?" he replied, swatting a few away from his face.

"You know what damned flies," I said, waving away the swarm around my head.

"Oh, these flies. They come from the chicken dung every farmer uses on his crops," he explained while brushing a swarm away from his face.

They were everywhere — even in the open shophouse-style restaurant where my Chinese friend took me to eat lunch. Having suddenly lost my appetite, I excused myself and wandered down the street, where I at last found some respite. It was an Indian restaurant, open-air like the Chinese restaurant, but hardly a fly in sight. A couple of bites of chicken explained why. The food was too hot and spicy for the flies — or me either, for that matter — to eat it.

Later when we started our first project in Malaysia's lowlands, I found chicken dung was also the most often used fertilizer in our area. The plague of flies seemed to follow me around the country, and I was determined to use something different on our vegetables.

"Mr. Loi, tell me about bat dung," I said one day when he and I were watching (and smelling) a gatherer unloading chicken dung.

Mr. Loi went into a long explanation about which Malaysian caves had the best deposits. "You can get all you want delivered here."

"How's the price?" I asked.

"Not too bad," Mr. Loi answered in typically vague Malaysian fashion.

"Find out for me. I think we might want to use it," I replied.

Nothing happened. I kept reminding him to find out. After several months, Mr. Loi showed me a couple of bags a gatherer brought for us to try. Then nothing further.

In desperation, I asked Dr. Oscar Opina, our technical manager, and Miss Wong, his assistant, to run scientifically controlled tests on several crops using different organic fertilizers. Oscar and Miss Wong applied bat dung in replicated plots side by side with chicken dung, as well as with some strange things like seaweed, an American lignite material, and a Japanese organic combination. The bat dung and chicken dung were by far the two best, but the bat dung gave significantly better plant growth than the chicken dung.

The whole exercise turned out to be useless. Mr. Loi insisted, "Chicken dung is what all Chinese farmers use and they make a lot of money. Some even have a Mercedes Benz."

Mr. Loi defined Malaysian-Chinese thinking in one sentence: tradition and profit. I felt like I was back in Georgia, where, as my grandfather had pontificated, "Farmers are as stubborn as the mules they plow."

Guano made in fertilizer plants gradually replaced manure on Southern farms since it was clean, easy to get, and didn't bring flies. Few people even remember "gu-anna" any more. Fertilizer is fertilizer, except to a few marketing geniuses who incorrectly call it plant food.

Momma used sheep manure in her gardens — which my bedroom window faced — so I was introduced to the pungent smell of Ramshorn Sheep Manure at an early age. After a few years the odor stopped bothering me; in fact, I rather grew to like it. It was a fantastic material and always made her plants (except asparagus) grow well. The producers of Ramshorn Sheep Manure and Longhorn Cattle Manure used a heating and dehydrating process to transform raw manure gathered in Chicago's massive stockyards into a light, fantastic organic fertilizer. It was a far cry from the heavy, almost useless, composted cow manure you find these days. I wish we still had Ramshorn Sheep Manure and Longhorn Cattle Manure, but they went by the wayside when the stockyards closed. I suppose the stockyards' neighbors and local environmentalists never liked the smell as much as I did.

The company's old offices in Atlanta were permeated with the scent of sheep and cow manure. We sold many railcar loads each year and kept huge stacks in an enclosed warehouse back of the offices. I didn't go there very often until we spent winters in Decatur, a suburb of Atlanta, where my sister and I went to school. On Saturdays, Dad made me take a streetcar to the office to insert catalogs in their mailing envelopes. The job was more boring than working in Momma's garden, but during the school year I didn't have the alternative of working in the nursery. The only thing nice about those Saturdays was the smell, which reminded me of home at Lovejoy.

One thing was certain: I would never get away from work at Hastings Seed Company; Dad believed unending toil was the only way to prepare a teenager for life on earth as well as to ensure a satisfactory hereafter.

Momma preferred to use sheep manure on most plants but used cottonseed meal around her acid-loving plants, like camellias, azaleas, and boxwood, one of her very favorite plants. When our foundation plantings were boxleaf holly, she hoped they would die so she could replace them with boxwood. Unfortunately, 5-10-5 "farm" fertilizer worked fine on the boxleaf hollies, so they defied her and kept on growing with complete inelegance. After many years, she talked Dad into ripping them out. Finally she had beautiful boxwood and an elegant foundation planting to which she gave her love and best care. That meant fertilizing with cottonseed meal.

We sat on the terrace in the cool of the evening listening to her extol the virtues of boxwood. "Just smell their fragrance," she said. I couldn't smell anything except cottonseed meal but agreed with her since the new boxwood made her so happy.

~

How and How Much?

A customer brought a dead azalea to the nursery when I first started to work there. A salesman looked at it, then handed it to me. "What do you think might have killed it?" he asked. I looked at it carefully but had no idea what caused its death.

"Better show it to Nelson," I said, and off we went to find Nelson Crist.

"When did you fertilize it?" Nelson asked.

The man looked a bit surprised and answered, "A few weeks ago, right after they bloomed, like everyone says to."

"Are they mulched?" Nelson asked.

"Yes," he replied.

"Did you pull the mulch back to fertilize?"

"Yes. Did I do wrong?" the man inquired.

"I wouldn't say that you were wrong, just unlucky," Nelson replied.

Nelson explained how the customer had placed the fertilizer on top of shallow feeder roots when he removed the mulch. In fact, we could still see the fertilizer clinging to the top roots. Azaleas are very shallow-rooted with lots of feeder roots near the surface. Usually, there's enough rain to keep fertilizer from harming the roots, but that year the May drought started early. There was just enough moisture to start the fertilizer working but not enough to move it away from the feeder roots near the surface.

"The best way to fertilize azaleas is to scatter it on top of the mulch," explained Nelson. Rain will move it through the mulch a little at a time. Remember, spring rains usually stop in mid-May soon after azaleas finish blooming and are supposed to be fertilized. Be prepared to water in the fertilizer whenever it is dry."

Loy Thomas was the vegetable expert at our Cheshire Bridge Road garden center when Betsy and I first moved to Sweet Apple and I started my own vegetable garden. He had grown vegetables for many years in his large garden and freely dispensed advice to customers as well as staff. Loy's experience in a home garden was indispensable since most of the other staff were urban dwellers with no vegetable experience or ex-farmers who were used to planting large acreages.

At first, my biggest problem at Sweet Apple was applying fertilizer. I didn't have a mule-drawn fertilizer distributor like I remembered from my nursery days, and I always seemed to use too little or too much when spreading it by hand. When I asked him, Loy happily shared his method with me.

"It's simple," he said. "Put your finger under the drain hole of an eight-inch pot, then fill it with fertilizer. It makes a great fertilizer distributor."

I adopted the method and gradually refined it by measuring the pace at which I should walk to place the right amount along the sides of a row of plants. Loy's technique was a garden edition of the big side-dressing rigs we used on crops in our overseas projects.

Mo Franklin, a good friend of mine at Cornell, returned to his native Illinois to run his father's corn and cattle operation. Several years after we had graduated, he visited Atlanta and we had dinner together. Mo described his farm in glowing terms. When I asked about fertilizing his corn, he replied, "I take soil samples to a commercial lab. I get a report that states the exact ratio of nitrogen, phosphorous, and potash I should use as well as a cost-effective schedule of how much to use. If I want a specific number of bushels per acre, the chart tells me how much fertilizer to use and its cost. The higher yields require incrementally higher amounts of fertilizer so I figure whether it is better to pay the extra amount or buy the corn on the futures market. I look at the market prices, then make my decision." My head was swimming. I didn't tell Mo, but I thought reducing farming to labs, charts, and market indexes was obscene. I held my tongue and wondered where the excitement and mystery in growing plants was headed.

Fertilizing is a necessary part of gardening and farming, especially in areas like the Piedmont South, where the land was ruined by cotton farming or is now being bull-dozed away by developers. We don't have enough nutrients in the ground to grow things well, so we must add fertilizer.

Many of my radio callers ended by asking about the proper "fertilization" of a plant or what they should "feed" it with. If the call came before 8:00 a.m., the halfway point of the show, I patiently explained that fertilization was when flowers were pollinated and feeding was what you did to babies when they were hungry. "Fertilizing, not fertilization, is the act of applying fertilizer nutrients around plants. We can't feed a plant. It feeds itself when it produces sugar during photosynthesis, the process all life on this planet depends upon. Farmers and gardeners aren't little bees pollinating plants, but growers nurturing their plants as best we can," I would say.

If the call came after 8:00 a.m., when I was getting tired, I would be much more testy, bemoaning the ignorance at universities whose extension bulletins constantly use the terms incorrectly. My contempt was also (and still is) directed at the "plant food" manufacturers who advertise "feeding" a plant every so often. My regular callers soon learned and would laugh when they used either term incorrectly. Unfortunately, extension services and fertilizer companies still haven't learned the correct usage, at least to my way of thinking. Small matter? Not to me. Incorrect terminology hinders understanding. It makes people think that feeding a plant with fertilizer is like feeding themselves when they are hungry; a little makes them feel pretty good but a lot makes them feel great. Unfortunately, over-fertilizing can be disastrous.

"I have a group of azaleas that were doing fine but suddenly started dying," the caller said one Saturday morning in May. My routine was to ask a series of questions which would lead to the crux of the problem even when, as in this case, I was pretty sure of the answer. Too many garden "experts" assume a solution without asking enough questions to get on the same wavelength with the person doing the asking. I've listened to many bad answers because callers and show hosts weren't thinking the same way.

My questions in this case were: "How long have they been planted? How big are they? How well are they growing? Did they bloom well?" She answered that they were a couple of years old, they were up to her knee, they looked puny, but they had bloomed well.

"Did you fertilize them after they bloomed?" I asked.

"Yes," she replied.

"What did you use and how much did you put around each plant?" I asked, getting a bit suspicious.

"They were so puny that I fed them with 10-10-10 and put two cups full around each one."

I flinched at the term "fed" and said, "I am afraid you put too much."

"But they looked so weak, I thought they needed more."

I explained that fertilizer wasn't food but nutrients and that she had probably damaged the roots so badly that the plant died.

"You can't stuff a plant with fertilizer like you stuff a goose with grain to make him fat and tasty," I ended.

"Damn," was all she said as she hung up.

Chris told me that some Cornell professors now use

the term "fertilization" instead of "fertilizing" and showed me the definitions in a new dictionary. I was horrified that my school now accepts such modernisms, but glad Dr. Curtis has passed on since he pitched a fit (and gave us a bad grade) when we used the term incorrectly.

Applying the right amount of fertilizer is easier on a few large plants than on a bed of flowers or a row of vegetables in the garden. It is trickier still on a field of many plants like cotton, corn, or vegetables like we had in our projects. Even though we had huge fertilizer rigs pulled by tractors with transmissions gauged to exact speeds, we had to watch the depth of the knives that determined where the fertilizer was placed. We could either kill seedlings with too much fertilizer or keep them from developing with too little, just by setting the rigs incorrectly.

When I was working in the nursery at Lovejoy, I learned fertilizer terminology: "side dressing" was placing fertilizer on one side of a row of plants; "top dressing" was placing fertilizer on top of seeds in a row before they germinated or, in the case of grain and lawn grasses, spreading it evenly over growing plants. In Egypt and Malaysia there was a third method of fertilizing we used in fields of vegetables. Germinating seedlings need fertilizer quickly so we placed it in the furrow before planting the seeds. I don't know what this was called, but it wasn't "under dressing," which sounds reasonable but might have had some bad connotations in a respectable project.

Jack Cope was one of the finest fertilizer manufacturers I have ever known. He kept up with the best nutrient sources and mixed his nutrients correctly and carefully, something that many blenders don't do. Jack's Reliance Fertilizer Company developed the Reliance brand, which included Reliance Rose Fertilizer, Reliance Azalea and Camellia Special, and Reliance Garden Fertilizer with minor elements, which was the first one I found stating the exact amount of each micronutrient rather than a mere mention of which ones were included. We liked Jack's use of organic materials like blood meal and cottonseed meal as sources of some of the nitrogen, phosphorous, and potash.

Before he sold Reliance and we sold Hastings, Jack blended two lawn fertilizers for us based on recommendations by Dr. Glenn Burton, the internationally famous grass scientist at the Georgia and United States Experiment Station at Tifton, Georgia. We introduced the first one in the fifties and the second one in the sixties. "Hastings Lawn Fertilizer" had 25 percent organic sources of the major nutrients, which made it last longer than most other lawn fertilizers. The second was "Hastings Turfgreen," which contained the new uramite form of nitrogen and lasted even longer. Its formula is now used for many lawn fertilizers. We never recommended "feeding" a lawn, like most fertilizer companies do, but gave recommended fertilizing rates (not fertilization rates).

The art of gardening includes understanding how much fertilizer to use around plants or on grass. Use rates have to be very general since there are so many different fertilizer formulas and so many different kinds of plants which have their own requirements. In Malaysia, I used a computer for the first time to figure application rates. Large farming areas here in the United States have local blenders who mix any formula you need, but in Malaysia, we could buy only a few set formulas, like 13-13-13 or 15-15-15. We could also buy ammonium nitrate with 32 percent nitrogen, potassium sulfate, and super phosphate which were pretty expensive. Taking the use rates for each vegetable we grew, along with the recommended application rates for the various fertilizers, I figured how much of each kind of fertilizer to mix together to get the proper formula. I could never have done it without a computer, even though it was an old Apple IIc. I wished for Mo Franklin's soil testing service and in my mind apologized to Mo for thinking these new farming practices were obscene.

~

Back to Nature?

Winter was a busy and interesting time at Hastings Seed Company. We mailed the spring catalog between Christmas and New Year's Day, and by mid-January orders started pouring in. Also, Northern businessmen came through in droves heading for Florida's sun like flocks of migrating birds. There was method in our sudden popularity. If these sun birds made a few calls, they could charge the trip as a business expense. Most were a joy to visit with, but more than a few were a pain in the neck since they had little interest in talking business, especially about problems we might have with their products. Fortunately for me, most of them wanted to see Dad or Elbridge Freeborn, whom they knew from trade association meetings.

Ours was an egalitarian company long before it was the thing to be. Money was tight when we had to relocate from Mitchell Street to our Marietta Street building, so little was done to the building before we moved in. The main office was in a big open room on the third floor where each department had a specific area with desks for the staff and manager. There were no partitions, so everyone was clearly visible. I thought the arrangement was archaic and pretty dumb since it was noisy and impossible to talk privately with a coworker or a visiting nurseryman. But as the most junior manager at the time, I had no say in the matter.

We could hear Dad when one of our least favorite sun birds arrived — a well-known business owner who was milking the organic gardening cow to death. His visits always started calmly, with Dad's Southern gentility still prevailing. But when the man started his "poisoning the earth" lectures, the shouting match was under way. Dad deeply resented the implication that he had no feeling for the land, having lived through two hideous farm depressions in the South during which he and my grandfather preached improving the land with green manures and good soil practices. The land was important to Dad for reasons greater than hitching his wagon to a new fad in order to make gobs of money.

Since Dad would always come over to let off steam after these arguments, I knew my day was shot.

"I asked him over and over how were we going to feed over two hundred million people with organically grown wheat and corn," Dad would tell me, as if I hadn't heard. "There's not enough manure in this country to grow millions of acres of grain. Besides, animal populations on the farm are declining rapidly since more and more farmers use tractors instead of horses and mules to plow and cultivate their crops. But he won't ever listen to facts like that."

Dad had a way of clearing his throat during a conversation, and more frequently when he was mad or excited. During Dad's soliloquies after these visits, he cleared almost as much as he talked. I would sit listening until he calmed down, cleared his throat a couple of final times, and left, having talked — and cleared — the anger out of his system.

In an earlier chapter I mentioned my visit with Dr. Yussef Wali, Egypt's Minister of Agriculture, at which he lamented Egypt's outmoded farming practices and stressed the importance of increasing his country's food production. After that meeting, as I went outside to find Hamdi, my driver, I was struck again — as all newcomers to Cairo are — by the enormous number of people you see. Cairo had an estimated population of fourteen million people packed along a narrow strip of land next to the Nile River. Over a million people lived in the City of the Dead, the ancient but still-used cemetery.

Hamdi was in a hurry to start home to Alexandria as quickly as possible to avoid rush hour congestion — as bad as any I have ever seen. We wound our way through the hideously snarled Cairo traffic to Giza, the home of the Great Pyramids, where the desert road to Alexandria begins.

The Great Pyramids rose before us like huge sentinels guarding entry into the Sahara Desert, which lies barren all the way to Libya. The throngs of people were soon gone. After about an hour, I could see nothing but sand on both sides of the road. I thought about Dr. Wali's remarks as Hamdi drove through the desert. How on earth could Egypt ever feed so many people with so little land, so many donkeys and buffaloes, and so few tractors? Obviously, they would have to maximize productivity like we were doing on our desert farm. With our tractors and high-grade fertilizers, we were producing thirty to forty tons of high-quality tomatoes, while the best farms in the rich Nile Delta produced only fifteen tons of marginal tomatoes.

I thought about Dad and the sun bird many years before. What if people like Dad's antagonist stopped the use of commercial fertilizers? What effect would it have on Egypt's efforts to reclaim the desert and make it productive? In a word, life in Egypt would become unbearable, and farm productivity everywhere would be crippled. It would mean returning to archaic farming methods. Work animals would consume half the crops our farms produce, and Americans would go to bed hungry, just like many Egyptians do.

The main advantage of longevity is having a broad perspective, if you don't succumb to being close-minded. I came into this world when manures and organic fertilizers were the mainstays in gardening and farming. By the time I finished college, farmers and gardeners used more inorganic (commercially made) than organic fertilizers. The "back-to-organic" farming and gardening movement started later, preaching that no fertilizer was good except when it came from an organic source.

Organic gardeners amuse me greatly with their vehement advocacy and immunity to reason. A caller to my radio show pounded on me about my advice to use ammonium nitrate on sweet corn. "You should never recommend poisoning the earth. There are many good organic sources of nitrogen," she said.

I asked her if she used nitrate of soda. "Goodness no. It's a poison. Nitrogen must come from organic matter like manure and blood meal to be safe," she responded emphatically.

"Then nitrate of soda from South America is okay, since it originally came from bird droppings," I calmly told her. She mumbled something about my being a wise joker and hung up.

We cannot go back to ancient practices, only forward, using every possible method to keep farm productivity rising. Otherwise our lives could become as bleak as the

Sahara Desert that Hamdi and I drove beside on our way to Alexandria. I hoped that barren land beside our route wasn't prophetic of the world's future, and, once again, I uttered a silent apology to Mo Franklin.

Chapter Seven

Pruning

*For before the harvest, as soon as the bud blossoms
And the flower becomes a ripening grape, Then He
will cut off the sprigs with pruning knives And remove
[and] cut away the spreading branches.*

— Isaiah 18:5
NASB

"Hey, there's a big ol' copperhead in here!" I yelled from inside the Burford holly hedge surrounding the lower garden. I was in there cutting off some cherry laurel seedlings that Momma noticed sprouting in her hedge.

She had found me sitting on a limb about halfway up my sweet gum tree and had told me to go find the big loppers and meet her in the garden. When I got there, she pointed toward the cherry laurel foliage showing among the Burford hollies and asked me to crawl in there and lop the sprouts off at the ground.

I crawled under the sticky holly branches, and she stuck the loppers through the hedge and pointed to the intruders. "Cut them as close to the ground as you can so they won't sprout again," she called.

I lopped away the ones she pointed to and was crawling on all fours looking for some more to cut when I saw the coiled snake.

When I hollered out, Momma quickly parted the branches and looked in.

"You sure it's a copperhead?"

"Yes'm, I'm danged sure."

Momma grabbed the branches and tried to get closer. The noise diverted the snake who shifted its focus to the rustling branches. I scooted away, plunged under the branches and into the garden, then flopped on the grass with my heart pounding a mile a minute. Momma yelled for Willie to bring a hoe to kill the snake, but by the time he got there the snake was gone.

"Where are the loppers?" Momma suddenly asked.

"I guess I left them in there," I replied hesitantly, knowing I was the only one small enough to crawl back in the center of the huge bushes to fetch them. "I'll get them if Willie promises that danged snake is gone."

"He's long gone. He was as scared as you," Willie

told me, looking at my face, still drained of color from the fright.

"You might as well cut the rest of the seedlings while you are in there," Momma said, peering through the branches. She was as practical as anyone I have ever known and would certainly have gone back in the thicket if she had been my size.

I didn't mind. The fact of the matter is that pruning has always been my cup of tea. When I was young, I dreamed of being a doctor like Dr. Joe Reed, our family surgeon and close friend. But medicine wasn't in my cards. Hastings Seed Company loomed too large in my future for me to have a chance at anything else. Pruning plants was the only surgery I was destined to perform.

Pruning is an ancient art dating back to biblical times when grape growers in the Holy Land learned to prune their vines to make them produce more high-quality fruit for making wine. The fermentation process killed the dysentery bacteria which often caused death, especially to infants. More grapes meant more wine and a better chance of escaping the stomach problems which resulted from drinking water or anything not fermented. The Europeans developed types of pruning, like shaping and espaliering, to make plants develop in unusual ways. Pears were pruned and trained against warm walls to protect their fruiting buds from winter damage and loss of the crop. The Japanese perfected the intricacies of root/top balancing in the ancient art of bonsai.

~

Tools

It takes knowledge, a love of adventure, courage, and determination to master the art of pruning. And it takes the proper tools. My friend Hubert Nicholson, the son of an English emigre, taught me much about pruning. Nick believed the old English adage, "Prune when your knife is sharp and keep your knife sharp all the time." But I must add, prune at the right time or your plant may be in trouble.

Europeans, especially the English, have many special shears and knives for different types of pruning, but American catalogs and nurseries usually list only loppers and a few standard shears, which may or may not be the right type.

Nobody should garden without a *good* pair of pruning shears — that means the knife-cut type, with the cutting blade that slides snugly back of a holding bar. That may seem like a minor point, but it is extremely important. When the blade is placed toward the inside of a plant, the cutting action removes any damaged tissue caused by the holding bar. Anvil shears are a disaster because the sharp blade lands in the middle of the holding bar, leaving a small crushed area on the plant. This damaged tissue can cause dieback and also provide an entrance for insects and diseases.

A couple of years ago, after we had returned from our years abroad and had refocused on growing things in the South, I was asked to write an article for a magazine. One day an intern with the magazine called to clarify some points I had made.

"What do you mean by knife-cut shears?" she asked.

I explained about the cutting blade sliding back of the holding bar and how important it was.

In a few days she called back and told me I was wrong. "What you are talking about is a scissor-cut pruning shear, not a knife-cut," she adamantly informed me.

"That makes no sense at all since the shears I am talking about have one knife and one holding bar, not two sharp blades like a pair of scissors," I said huffily.

"I am replacing knife-cut with scissor-cut since a local nursery expert said that's the correct name. He said there's no such thing as a knife-cut shear."

I took a deep breath and replied, "If you don't mind being wrong, put whatever you want."

I have learned over my many years that some battles are worth fighting and some are not. This one was not.

I chalked up her obstinacy to the old saying, "Ignorance is bliss."

On a trip to England, Betsy and I visited our friend Geoffrey Greer, the managing director of Wilkinson Sword Garden Tools. The factory was an ancient-looking edifice with machinery which befit its appearance. Being a good American used to shiny modern plants and equipment, I felt betrayed. How had Wilkinson earned its reputation for producing the finest garden tools in the world? My confidence was fully restored when I saw the skill and care with which each pair of blades and each set of handles was crafted. The ancient machinery remained for a purpose. It prevented the metal from heating too much when stamping out the blades, thus preserving the temper. Over thirty years have passed since I bought my first Wilkinson shears. They still sharpen to a fine edge and work like a charm.

Like so many family-owned manufacturing companies, Wilkinson Sword Ltd. is now gone after being sold and resold several times. I suppose it took family owners who carefully and correctly passed the port wine after lunch in the wood-panelled board room to understand the formula for the company's success: a good reputation assures profitability.

∾

Drastic Measures

Soon after we opened our Cheshire Bridge Road garden center in Atlanta, we began weekend instructional classes on various gardening subjects. I wanted to add classes on growing fruits in the backyard, and since none of us were experts on pruning fruit trees, I asked Hubert Nicholson to be our instructor. Nick was an expert on both ornamentals and fruit trees, but his lectures on pruning fruits excited me the most. He had a gift for teaching precise horticultural methods while using layman's terms, and he always drew big crowds. After his talk, Nick would wander around the nursery answering questions.

One Sunday afternoon after a demonstration, Nick was in the nursery when a man with a six-foot-tall, bare-root peach tree stopped him. "I missed your talk but the man over there said you would prune this for me anyway," he said, pointing to a salesman.

Nick agreed, then proceeded to cut off the six-foot tree about two feet above the planting mark. The man's eyes just about popped out of his head.

"Now do you want me to explain why I pruned it that way?" Nick asked.

"You'd better, 'cause if you don't explain it real good, I want my money back," the man answered.

Nick gave a short version of peach tree pruning theory, starting with cutting off a tree severely, then making new sprouts develop a wide open head where more fruiting branches can develop. In a very few minutes, Nick demonstrated the ancient art of training by pruning.

"Peaches grow naturally into an upright tree with a single trunk," Nick explained. "Last summer's shoots produce this year's fruit, so you want as much new growth each year as possible. If left to grow upright, the tree will produce fruit on the outer branches, some so high up they are hard to pick. Orchardists try to make the tree grow wide, rather than tall, so the producing shoots are more numerous than when the tree grows naturally."

The man smiled broadly, paid for the tree and left.

Nick laughed and said, "I thought we were going to lose a sale and a peach tree."

~

Tree-topping

My mother loved to prune. She grabbed a pair of pruning shears almost every time she went to the garden. She snipped a long vine here or an awkward branch there, leaving little piles of clippings around the garden for me to rake in a pile and for Willie to haul away in his wheelbarrow. When we had company, she took florist clippers to snip flowers for the guests as they drifted from one garden to another.

From her I learned not to leave the loppers in the holly hedge. I also learned — the hard way — that you should never top a shade tree.

Our house was situated in a frame of two huge tulip poplars, which had sprouted many years before in the War-Between-the-States trench that had once run through what was now our front lawn. Momma wanted two *Magnolia grandiflora* trees as evergreens in the frame, but they had to be in exactly the right spots. She stood on the edge of the lawn, positioning herself directly in front of the entrance to the house, while Dad and I acted as trees. When Momma had us in just the right spot, we both drove a stake in the ground where we stood. That's where Willie planted her new magnolias.

They were her pride and joy. She had heard that the best way to make a magnolia really grow was to bury a dead cow nearby. When none of our cows volunteered for this duty, she nurtured the trees with barnyard manure, which proved an effective alternative.

The young trees had just started to grow well when some of my school friends came for a visit. They were city boys who weren't the least bit interested in looking for Civil War bullets or climbing in barn lofts, so we decided to play baseball on the front lawn. Unfortunately and to my everlasting consternation, a long fly ball knocked out the top of one of the little magnolia trees. Momma was mad as a hornet, but Dad assured her that it would still develop just fine. I assured her, too, hoping like everything that Dad was really correct. He wasn't and I wasn't.

The two trees grew huge over the years, but the one with the top knocked out always looked funny — like an old-fashioned rabbit-ears TV antenna. Until the day she died, Momma never tired of explaining to visitors just exactly why that magnolia looked so odd. I guess that hearing the story told so often made the point sink in.

I certainly remembered it vividly years later at Sweet Apple — and sympathized with Momma's anger — when I arrived home one afternoon while the EMC pruning crew was "protecting the power lines" and doing a real number on some of my pine trees.

I found the supervisor and asked why on earth they were butchering my trees. "Don't you know if you cut the limbs that way, they'll die, and then borers will come in and kill my trees?"

After a long argument, I finally made him sign a statement that when my pines died, the EMC would take them down at no cost to me. They died, of course, and it almost took an act of Congress to make them come back and take them out — even with my written promise from their tree "expert." The removal crew got a big kick out of the whole thing. They saw right away that their expert had made a bonehead move and congratulated me for having made him sign that letter.

I don't know how many times Chris and I wrote "never top a shade tree" in our book, *Month by Month Gardening in the South*. My past painful experiences made me want to emphasize the point over and over again.

~

Flowers

Timing is always an important element in pruning, but especially in pruning plants that have flowers.

Nelson Crist had a way of tying gardening practices to important events in our lives, as I learned during a discussion of hybrid roses. I had learned at Cornell to prune them in the late fall, so I was confused when Dad recommended pruning in the spring.

"You have to prune them like your Dad says," Nelson advised me. "If you prune in the fall, they will sprout too early during a warm spell in the winter. The plant has a large root system, so it tries to replace its top as soon as the weather warms. New shoots develop rapidly but way too early since there is still a chance that a hard freeze will kill them," Nelson explained.

"So what's the best time to prune?" I asked.

"On March 15 at ten o'clock in the morning," he replied without hesitation.

"Why so specific?" I asked, laughing at the absurdity.

"When you tell someone to prune in early March, they won't really understand the importance of timing. But if I tell them to prune at ten o'clock in the morning on March 15, they will have just filed their income taxes and that means two things. They'll be so mad they'll prune severely, which is very important, and they'll prune late enough to prevent freeze damage."

I remember Nelson's explanation and use it frequently when lecturing or writing about roses. Now we file our taxes on April 15, which is much too late, but telling Nelson's story makes people remember the two most important points about pruning roses: prune severely and prune late enough to make sure that hard freezes won't kill succulent new shoots.

One spring day I spotted some beautiful snowball shrubs, *Viburnum opulus*, by the side of the road in a well-kept landscape surrounding an idyllic country home. The next time I was going that way I took my camera in hopes of getting some good pictures. I pulled in the drive and introduced myself to a delightful lady who graciously invited me to take all the pictures I wanted. I noticed that the beautiful flowering specimens were all on one side of the drive while the snowball plants on the other side had no flowers.

After a tour around her yard, I was headed back to my car when I took a last, curious look at the nonblooming snowballs.

"Why don't they bloom like the others?" she asked.

"I'm not sure, but it might be that you pruned them a bit too late last summer," I cautiously replied. I didn't want to step on any toes since she was doing me a favor by letting me take pictures.

She looked puzzled, then said, "You know, that might be the problem. They grew a lot last year so we might have pruned them later than we should so we could see cars coming when we started out the driveway."

I explained that some plants, like her crape myrtles, set bloom buds on current growth and some, like her snowballs, set bloom buds on growth produced the previous summer. "These snowballs set buds last summer before you pruned, so you probably pruned them off," I told her.

The principle is so simple that few horticulture books ever bother to mention when a plant sets its buds — even though it is extremely important. The time you prune determines whether or not you will have future flowers . . . and fruits. Plants like dogwood, azaleas, *Camellia japonica*, and *Camellia sasanqua* have large buds that are easy to see, but the trick is to realize that when you see them, that's it. No more will be set until next year, so don't prune them off. Pruning before the buds are evident but after the tiny bud initial has started to develop is just as bad as pruning off nice plump buds.

Nelson Crist told me a good way to decide when to prune a flowering shrub. "If a plant blooms *before* the first of June, buds are set on last summer's growth, so wait until after it blossoms to prune. If it blooms *after* the first of June, buds are set on new growth, so prune them in the winter or early spring to force the growth on which flowers will come."

Over the years I have found Nelson's rule of thumb to be pretty good; however, gardening rules can't be depended on 100 percent of the time. For instance, some rhododendrons bloom after the first of June yet set their bloom buds the previous summer, so you have to wait until after they bloom to prune. Also, the first-of-June rule becomes "later in June" the farther north you go.

The worst grade I ever got in a class at Cornell was on a snap test in a Plant Physiology class taught by Dr. Curtis. The true and false questions looked so simple that all of us finished the twenty questions in a few minutes. Dr. Curtis told us to exchange papers and grade each other. The paper I graded had eight or ten correct answers, mine had about the same, and a boy nearby had even fewer.

I still remember one of the questions. True or false: chlorophyll is necessary for photosynthesis in plants. Everybody put true, but the answer was false. Dr. Curtis told us an exception, then said, "When dealing with living organisms like plants, never say never or never say always. There are exceptions to every rule."

The test didn't cause me to fail the course, but the lesson I learned has stuck with me for over half a century.

~

Evergreens

Boxwoods were Momma's pride and joy, not only in front of the terrace but throughout the gardens, where she used them to outline her flower beds. Thanks to her generous application of cottonseed meal, they grew beautifully. In fact they began to grow too big. By August one year, they were so overgrown and unsightly that they crowded her prize begonias and other annuals. They needed trimming badly.

Momma was a person of action, so she and Willie drastically trimmed the boxwood borders. They looked great until new growth started in September; it was a sickly yellow and made her borders look ridiculous. Dad and I inspected them carefully but found no reason for their funny color except the possibility that trimming so late had caused the problem. The funny yellowish growth turned pure white when the first frost formed in the garden. Momma was just sick.

I visited Karl Johnson, a studious nurseryman friend near Savannah, soon after the plants developed white tops. I asked Karl if he had ever heard of such a thing. He hadn't, but theorized that the days were getting shorter when Momma pruned. The new growth started near the time of the fall equinox when the day length was too short for good nutrient uptake "The plants should be converting sugar to starch to store for the winter, not using sugar for new growth," Karl said.

Karl's was the best explanation I ever heard for Momma's strange boxwood problem. After that, Momma pruned her boxwood by the Fourth of July. They never turned white again.

I gave many talks to the garden clubs that we regularly invited to meet at the garden centers. One winter night I was giving a talk on pruning when a lady asked if it was a good time to prune pine trees. I told her it was a great time since the sap was down.

She said, "That's what I told my husband, but he said I didn't know what I was talking about. He said you needed to prune when the sap was up and not down."

"I think you were right," I said.

"I thought I was right and told him the only sap around when it's cold was him." Everybody howled with laughter.

~

Catharsis

Plants develop a balance between their roots and top. When either is disturbed, like when you prune the top, a plant immediately tries to replace what has been cut away. In this way pruning acts a lot like fertilizing because it makes plants grow. The art of pruning is to make the new growth better than the old. Fertilizing after pruning aids the new growth, so usually they are done one after the other.

Clematis is one of my favorite plants, but in the old days few of us in the mid-South grew any but the dark, blue-purple Jackman, which was tough and floriferous. Even using my mother's inverted-pot practice for keeping the roots cool and shaded, hot summer days in the piedmont South were not what clematis liked . . . or so I thought.

One Sunday after church, I spotted a clematis with big white flowers growing on a mailbox in the Buckhead area of Atlanta. It was spectacular — dark green foliage, huge blossoms, and the vine compactly growing around and over the mailbox. I had to stop and inspect this gorgeous plant. Why was it doing so much better than virtually any I had ever seen in Atlanta?

Frank Smith, the noted Atlanta nurseryman, had the answer, "Prune a hybrid clematis to the ground every three years. Prune it back some every year. Then fertilize it with bonemeal to make it grow and keep the soil sweet."

I had to try a clematis at Sweet Apple. The first one never got going because our dog dug it up while scratching in the bonemeal. I tried again, but this time I used limestone and 10-10-10 fertilizer instead of bonemeal. Momma's inverted-pot invention kept the roots cool so it grew like a weed and soon covered the pole it was planted on. I pruned it heavily each winter, perhaps more than Frank recommended, so I never had to do the drastic pruning every third year. My clematis was beautiful for many years until we moved overseas. Unfortunately, a young puppy decided it would be fun to pull it down and drag it around the yard.

Aristotle used the term catharsis for the effect of a tragic drama on an audience. It purges one's emotions. Pruning is a catharsis for me. I do my best pruning when I am riled or overwrought. My tensions go away and sleep comes easily during the night. If I can develop a prescription for pruning, maybe I can be a doctor after all.

Chapter Eight

Pestilences

When you find a poisonous plant in the woods, within a few steps you will see its antidote.
— Indian Proverb

I was twelve years old the summer before the Japanese attacked Pearl Harbor. My friends and I closely followed the German progress across Europe and worried what would happen if the Germans invaded America. We talked a lot about the war.

One morning in late August, I woke up to a strange rhythmical humming sound, first loud and then soft. Rolling over on my bed toward the window, I saw clouds of smoke coming from the source of the strange noise. Being only half awake, I knew it must have something to do with the the war. The cloud slowly drifted toward the house and into my window; my eyes began itching and I started sneezing. In the words of my Malaysian-Chinese friends, "It scared me to hell."

I ran downstairs in my pajamas and found Dad sitting at the table calmly eating breakfast. "What's going on?" I asked excitedly.

"What's going on with what?" he replied, hardly looking up.

"All that gas and smoke and noise," I said, getting even more agitated.

"Oh, that. Wes (as Dad called Mr. Watts) sent some men over to dust the Sweet Autumn clematis for beetles. They are eating up the foliage."

"What's that funny smell?" I asked.

"Sabadilla dust. It's good for killing beetles," he said, then started eating again.

I ran upstairs, quickly dressed, and tore back downstairs and out to the garden to see this strange sight first hand. Bennie slowly turned the handle of a big Hudson duster, which spewed a cloud of sabadilla dust all over the massive vines covering the trellis that made a semi-circle in back of the pool garden. I wanted to watch but the dust made me sneeze, so I went back inside and ate with Dad. The immediate threat of an invasion by the Germans was over.

After breakfast, Dad took me to see if Bennie's effort

had paid off. It had. Dead beetles were everywhere. We had won that war, anyway.

"What is sabadilla dust?" I asked.

"It comes from the seeds of a member of the lily family in Central America. It controls many beetles, like Mexican bean beetles, which rotenone won't kill," Dad explained. He showed me a red bag with a big picture of the devil and the words "Red Devil Dust" on the front.

"Sabadilla is hard to find, but I found a man in Mobile who imports the seeds and manufactures the dust. It really works well," Dad added.

Insects and diseases that attack plants are a big part of life when you grow up in the country, especially on a working farm. We had to control boll weevils, bean beetles, squash bugs, bag worms, and diseases like Black Spot which attacked our fields of roses. This was before DDT and a whole generation of more powerful insecticides and fungicides were introduced after World War II. In my early days, most insecticides came from parts of plants — like rotenone from derris or cube roots; pyrethrin from the flowers of pyrethrum, a member of the same genus as Momma's chrysanthemums in the garden; and sabadilla from seeds of the Central American lily.

We occasionally used arsenic and nicotine sulfate from tobacco plants, but both were horribly poisonous and dangerous to handle, so Dad used them only as a last resort. I wished, perhaps foolishly, that he would relent and use arsenic to kill those nasty bagworms Mr. Watts made us pick off the juniper bushes. I was convinced arsenic poisoning couldn't be as bad as picking those worms on hot Saturday mornings, but Dad's caution prevailed.

The only two fungicides I remember using in those days were basic copper and sulfur. Fortunately, the *multiflora* rose understock we budded on was not susceptible to Black Spot, but the fields we budded the previous year could be seriously damaged by the disease. Mr. Watts had them dusted regularly with sulfur, when the weather wasn't so hot it would burn the leaves. Sulfur controlled the Black Spot, but it smelled up the area pretty badly. I was thankful that *multiflora* was resistant to Black Spot so we didn't have to bud plants that smelled like rotten eggs.

We also grew many acres of wheat, which was susceptible to a rust disease. Dad thought fighting it with fungicides was too difficult and expensive. Instead, he banned barberries — the host plant — from the farm. He wouldn't even let Momma plant any barberry cultivars in the garden, which was fine with me since their needle-like thorns made rose thorns look wimpy.

~

Nature's Way

In those days, boll weevils were the most infamous insect in the South. The boll weevil invasion in the 1920s devastated the South's cotton crops and left many farm families close to starvation. Our company suffered in turn because farmers had so little money to spend on seeds and supplies. My grandfather preached planting other cash crops, but stubborn Southern farmers kept planting cotton and kept losing their crops.

By my time, there was some help from insecticides. The most unusual was arsenic mixed in molasses, which Dad's friend M. H. Elder used. M. H., Jr., and I would ride our ponies to the cotton field and watch workers dip swabs in the gooey mixture and dab a glob on each boll. Somehow it worked fairly well, if a rain didn't come along and wash off the mixture before the boll weevils were killed.

The boll weevil, along with farms too small to have picking machines, killed cotton production in Georgia. By the time I first went overseas in 1979, a cotton field was as rare in Georgia as an old-fashioned grist mill. King Cotton had done its damage to Georgia's land and moved on to the Mississippi Delta, Texas, and California.

In fall of 1993, I drove to Tifton, Georgia, to discuss our insect problems in Malaysia with vegetable expert Dr. David Adams. As I drove southward from Sweet Apple past Macon, I could not believe my eyes: all around me lay vast fields white with open cotton, and convoys of huge picking machines clattered down the back roads.

"What happened to the boll weevil?" I asked David.

He explained that farmers now controlled boll weevils by releasing sterile males into the population. As a result, the boll weevil population had practically disappeared. Altering an insect's biological processes to prevent it from reproducing was taking pest control in a new and formidable direction.

King Cotton returned to Georgia, but modern farmers are wiser than those in the thirties. Cotton areas are now farther south where fields are large and land is flat. Big tractors prepare and plant large acreages quickly, irrigation keeps plants from struggling in droughts, and mechanical picking accomplishes in a few weeks what used to take from late August until frost. Rural children no longer start school at the beginning of August, then take off until cotton harvesting was over. King Cotton returned, but no longer ruled over rural life.

By the time I started gardening at Sweet Apple, there were chemicals to control insects, diseases, *and* weeds.

But some pests, like cabbage green worms (we call them loopers) couldn't be controlled with regular garden chemicals. I read about a new biological control called *Bacillus thuringiensis*, nicknamed BT, which was supposed to wipe out cabbage worms. It was fabulous! It also did a great job on other soft worms, like tomato horn worms and fruit worms, as well as those pesky worms that sometimes ate up Betsy's geraniums.

Another reason I started looking for alternatives to chemical controls was all the talk about Agent Orange after the Vietnam War. I had used a lot of 2-4-5T, which was similar to Agent Orange, on the underbrush in my woods, but its notoriety scared me so badly that I stopped using what I had and bought no more.

About this same time, Elbridge Freeborn pointed us toward another kind of biological control — praying mantises and lady beetles, which he wanted to sell through the mail order department and in our stores. I carefully set out the mantis cases in my garden (each of which held a hundred or so eggs that were supposed to hatch when placed on a plant outside) and let loose droves of live lady beetles. But the mantis eggs never hatched, and the lady beetles disappeared without eating nearly enough of the spider mites and other insects I was trying to get rid of. I came to the conclusion that gardeners must be pragmatic. I used chemicals carefully when nothing else saved my plants from excessive damage. The rest of the time I tried every biological control I could find.

~

Lost Battles

Of course, the war against insects and diseases can never be won for good. The best we can hope for is to hold our own one skirmish at a time, and even this modest aspiration is often frustrated.

When I was on my way to Southeast Asia for the first time in 1987, my friend Fred Burns asked me to look for sources of pyrethrin, a major botanical insecticide used in household sprays. I knew pyrethrin was grown in a few select places in Africa and South America but didn't know it was grown in Asia. Fred told me he had once imported pyrethrin from Papua New Guinea.

"Pyrethrin from Papua New Guinea is the best quality in the world, but its export has almost stopped. See what you can find out. I can sell a huge amount," he told me.

Neither Fred nor I had any concept of the vast distances between countries in the Pacific. He thought it would be an easy trip from Manila or Kuala Lumpur to Papua New Guinea, so he thought I could pop down there for a day or two. As it turned out, it was many hours flying time away and hard to get to, but I told Fred I would keep an eye out.

After our project started in Malaysia, I was approached by an enterprising Chinese banker who was starting branches in several other Pacific Rim markets. He wanted to open a bank in Port Moresby, the capital of PNG, the quid pro quo being that he would help the government solve some of their agricultural problems. He asked me to go to PNG with a mutual friend to take a look, and I agreed — with pyrethrin and Fred Burns in the back of my mind.

We made the long trip to Port Moresby, where we were met by two lawyers who were helping obtain the bank's approvals. They agreed that the best agricultural potential was in the highlands and also noted that the commercial production and extraction of pyrethrin was a top priority of the government. We flew to Mt. Hagen in the highlands, and from there would drive to Wabaq, the center of production. Our new Port Moresby lawyer friends went with us and acted as our driver and guide; one was native to the area and spoke the local dialect, and the other was an Australian who had lived in PNG since before independence. We would have gotten nowhere without them.

The ride was memorable — through beautiful farm

land and spectacular mountain and valley vistas — but on the single gravel road that ran between major towns, travel was slow, even in our four-wheel-drive, twin-cab pickup truck. It slowed further when we came to a collapsed bridge and our truck had to inch down a muddy bank to a swift mountain stream, then be pulled up the other side by several dozen men with a huge rope. I was amused to see that every other vehicle had to pay twice to get across, once before going down, the other after coming up the other side. But we were honored guests because our driver/lawyer friend was from the tribe in the area.

Near Wabaq I found beautiful farm land. The area was high, cool, and flat, ideal for mechanical production using large tractors. There was ample water for irrigation and unrestricted boundaries for future growth. I decided the land was suitable for vegetables, cattle, chickens, and almost any other crop you could think of — including pyrethrin. We saw many small plots growing beautifully but being harvested by hand. I visualized larger fields with mechanical or it least better-organized harvesting. Such a project would help satisfy the crying need for the safe insecticide, and at the same time bring significant income into the area.

But, as always, there was a problem, which I discovered when we visited the pyrethrin processing plant in

Mt. Hagen. It seemed that Mt. Hagen, the site of the processing plant, and Wabaq, where the plant was cultivated, were in two different tribal areas and the tribes didn't get along at all. In fact, they still battled each other with axes. "Why?" I asked.

"Any number of reasons — like the theft of a pig or snatching a wife or kidnapping a young girl of marriage age," one companion replied.

There was no way they would cooperate, at least at the time I was there, and that was the end of the matter.

The Chinese herbal legacy spreads throughout most of Asia, and during my Asian experience I always kept an eye out for herbs and plant derivatives that rural people used as cures and pest control measures. We tried many at our project, including a natural virus which attacks a green worm on okra.

Dr. Kitti Vitoonvitlak, our advisor from Thailand and the owner of a fabulous toxic-free vegetable project, demonstrated the virus to us. He showed our managers how to harvest the dying worms, grind them up, and make a solution to spray the okra leaves.

We had two problems: first, we never had enough spray; and, second, when we used what little we had, the worms ate too many leaves before they died. Another good idea down the drain.

When I was on a trip home from Malaysia for a month or so, I got a call from John Huyck, our farm manager in Egypt and later at our first project in Malaysia. The last time I had talked to John he was in the Dominican Republic growing cantaloupe and hot pepper. Now he was growing genetic hybrid potatoes in India. I suddenly remembered that India was a major source of Neem, a remarkable insect repellent and control I had just been reading about.

"You ever heard of a natural material called Neem? It comes from the leaves of the Neem tree," I told John.

"Never heard of it, but I'll check around," John replied. "We got all kinds of trees I haven't ever seen before. Maybe one of them is Neem."

John called back in a few days to say, "We got Neem trees all around." He then launched into a very long story about having burned his hand on a hot exhaust pipe, and how the lady who cooked for him cured it with a poultice made by boiling the leaves from a tree in the yard.

"I asked what the stuff was and found out it was Neem," John explained.

This was great. Not only was I excited about finding a commercial source of Neem our for our project in Malaysia, but Fred Burns was interested in importing it. John's response? His potato project took up all of his time. He couldn't help me.

Back at Sweet Apple, by the way, I have found Neem to be an effective control against whitefly. I first use insecticidal soap, which kills the adults, then Neem to prevent the immature wingless insects from developing into flying adults. It takes awhile, and sometimes leaves are damaged before the process works, but this combination works better than anything else I use.

My father used to quote an old Indian saying: "When you find a poisonous plant in the woods, within a few steps you will see its antidote." I kept searching for natural antidotes to pest problems, whether in my overseas projects or in my garden at Sweet Apple.

～

Tomato Wars

I love to grow tomatoes in my garden, and in the early days I set aside an area where I planted thirty-six plants each year. I surely didn't need that many tomatoes, but I wanted to test new cultivars, like the famous hybrid Big Boy, to see how they performed alongside my favorites like Manalucie. I wanted to know when something new was better than an old favorite, like Dad had done with his huge vegetable trials many years before.

Geneticists were developing a whole new class of

tomatoes called VFN types, because they were resistant to Fusarium and Verticillium Wilts as well as nematodes, the microscopic insect that attacks and ruins tomato roots. My tomato patch was perfect for testing disease and nematode resistance since I grew tomatoes in the same spot year after year. Any susceptible cultivars would quickly die. I felt my trials were a success, not only as a means to offering better cultivars in the company but, as it turned out, as wonderful preparation for our project in Egypt, which grew so many hundreds of acres of tomatoes for the markets of the world.

But one problem that had escaped the notice of plant scientists was Blossom End Rot, a black corky condition found on the blossom end of tomato fruit. It was widespread on tomatoes in both home gardens and commercial fields. Everybody seemed to have a different explanation: too much water, too little water, poor moisture holding capacity in the soil, and on and on.

One day as I was browsing through the latest volume of the proceedings of the American Society of Horticultural Science, I came upon a paper on controlling Blossom End Rot. Scientists had discovered that the condition was caused by a calcium deficiency in the plant, and they had corrected it with a calcium solution.

All of us at the company were delighted. We showed the article to a friend of ours who was a small chemical formulator, and his formula was ready for sale the next year. We recommended a fall or early spring application of limestone followed by a spray of the Blossom End Rot elixir when any black-bottomed fruit showed up. Finally the problem of Blossom End Rot was solved.

But some problems on tomatoes had no answers from either biological or chemical control measures. At a company meeting back in the sixties Elbridge Freeborn read us a report on a hideous new tomato disease called Bacterial Wilt for which there was no control. Vegetable specialists advised simply removing any infected plant from the garden, being careful not to touch any healthy ones.

It was a really frightening scenario, and the company was deeply concerned about this new menace. One evening after dinner I made my regular stroll through the garden and was "scared to hell" when I saw a large tomato plant with tip wilt despite heavy rains a few days before. I dreaded the thought of an invasion of Bacterial Wilt, so I carefully dug the plant and took it to our homemade incinerator, where I closely inspected the lower stem for the white liquid which could be squeezed out of an infected stem. Nothing happened. I squeezed some more . . . nothing happened. I decided to look inside the stem to see what was going on, so I slit it open with my knife. I found the culprit! It was a stem borer, not an attack of bacteria. I was so happy that it wasn't Bacterial Wilt I would have shaken the worm's hand in delight at seeing him, if the poor fellow had a hand to grab. Instead, I just smushed him with my heel.

In the Philippines, Bacterial Wilt reared its ugly head again when my Filipino partners decided to try some tomatoes. I wasn't too enthusiastic, having found Bacterial Wilt to be indigenous in Asian tropical soils, but Melchor Tan, the project manager, brought supposedly resistant cultivars from Mindanao, and I brought some strongly VFN resistant cultivars from home. The warm moist weather caused the plants to grow rapidly and vigorously. Bal Balesteros, our technical manager, kept warning of the certain advent of Bacterial Wilt, but my own hopes were rising.

Over the years I have found that having confidence is half the battle. When Bal suddenly discovered tip wilting in a few isolated plants, he and the workers were certain it meant the end of our tomato efforts and wanted to pull up and burn every tip-wilted plant. Remembering my scare at Sweet Apple, I had an idea.

I wore a belly pack to carry pens, a notebook, and assorted other stuff including a small bottle of an elixir that was supposed to sterilize water. I asked one of our brightest workers, Joemarie Galve, to fetch a gallon of water, into which I squeezed the correct number of drops, then added a few more for good measure.

"What's that," Joemarie asked as I added the elixir.

"It'll kill the wilt," I said with such authority that I almost believed myself.

It turned out that some of our plants were wilting from lack of water in the hot Philippine sun, so our elixir was a miracle tonic. A few others had pythium stem disease — still easy to overcome and no reason to go pulling up good plants.

~

Detective Work

That project in the Philippines was beset by more insects and diseases than I have ever encountered anywhere in the world. We had every pestilence I had ever heard about and a few I didn't know existed. I thought I had bad problems with worms in my corn at Sweet Apple, but our project's first Silver Queen, which is usually somewhat resistant, was riddled. Bal Balesteros organized a squad of young Filipino workers to go through the rows of Silver Queen corn, carefully open the nose of each shuck, and extract the worms. This didn't seem particularly efficient to me, so I organized spray crews. One day as I was watching them walk down the rows pumping away with the backpack sprayers, I noticed the moths flying away and landing in the wild shrubs surrounding the field. We got much better control after I instructed them to spray the bushes around the field.

In Egypt the worst problem we encountered was severe mildew attacks on our cantaloupes. Jim Hunt, our packing manager, discovered the reason. The Nile delta farmers grew huge numbers of a certain type of squash for their delicious seeds instead of the flesh. Jim noticed that these squash plants would be covered with mildew when the fruit ripened. The farmers didn't mind because the mildew-infected fruits died and dried up quickly, making the seeds easy to extract.

We developed an early warning system using crew members who drove the delta road to Alexandria. They were instructed to watch the fields of squash for the first sign of mildew and report it to John Huyck, the farm manager. John, in turn, immediately organized an intensive spray program on our cantaloupes to prevent mildew damage. It worked.

Keeping plants healthy is a major part of gardening as well as farming. Once your plants are growing, then you have to become a good detective. You must watch your plants for changes, then carefully examine the victim, identify the suspected culprit, and finally devise a method of bringing the plant back to good health.

John Huyck is one of the best-organized farm managers I have ever known. His programs were always practical rather than academic and not always systematic like modern farmers think they should be. I had read about how to organize scouting programs to search out insect and disease problems in commercial vegetable fields. Such programs made a lot of sense to me, but when I told John we should start a scouting program, he didn't seem too enthusiastic. "That's for managers who don't like to get out in the field in the heat," he huffed.

As it turned out, John not only walked through every field every day, but made his supervisors walk through each of their fields every day. They made their foremen do the same. When anybody saw a problem with plants in their field, they reported it to the next higher up. In effect, John had devised his own scouting program.

John also had "the Little General," a desert boy who had green eyes and claimed his father was a British general. Well, the British generals were long gone by the time the boy was born, but John addressed him by the name he had chosen. The Little General was a born leader and soon ruled the other boys who fixed the drip irrigation tubes. Each one was assigned a block in a field and given a little belly pack in which to carry his tools and wires. The boys stayed in the field all day long watching for the sudden geyser which indicated a broken tube. Then they hustled over to the spot and repaired the break. John told the Little General what plant problems to look for and to tell the other boys. The Little General's army was John's last line of defense against plant problems. They reported any new insects and disease to the Little General, who bypassed the foreman and went straight to John.

"He's my kind of scout," John told me.

The natural sequence of events with plants, no matter what the type, is to choose what you want to grow, plant it the best you know how, and help it do what you want it to, which to me is where the fun begins. I call it nurturing a plant.

Discovering sick or dead plants in my garden or in our commercial projects is an affront which makes me angry. I think to myself, "Why did I let them get sick and die? I should have been clever enough to overcome these problems."

I am much harder on myself when the problems are at Sweet Apple, an attitude I came by naturally. It started when I was a small boy sitting on a fence watching Dad walk a field looking for poorly growing plants or pest attacks. He made meticulous notes, then met with the farm managers, Alf, Wes, and Ruben, to devise a strategy to overcome the problem. Later, I hated to see a customer bring a dead plant to the nursery, especially when its death was caused by sloppy planting or neglect.

Overall, though, I suppose I've been lucky. At least I haven't had to do battle with the kind of pestilence that killed entire populations and altered the course of history. I'm reasonably certain that such devastations were caused by crop-devouring insects or disease attacks on food-producing plants — either worm or wilt. What I don't know is whether such calamities are rightly to be attributed to angry gods. Again, I'm lucky: that's a question for those in the fields of religion and philosophy, not horticulture.

Epilogue

"Mr. Hastings, you have an overseas call from your wife."

I was getting ready for bed in my hotel room in Kuantan, Malaysia, when the phone rang. Back home it was very early morning, Betsy's and my witching hour for catastrophe, so I worried as the operator made the connection.

"Don, I didn't know whether to call and tell you or wait until you got home, but I decided to call. The house at Floweracres burned last night."

"Don't worry about me," I told her with honest conviction. "I'm happy, not sad. It's like shooting a broke-leg horse to put it out of its misery."

If it hadn't burned down, the house might have been renovated into a clubhouse — or who knows what. Since my mother had died in 1987 and my father moved to town, I hated driving by on US 19-41. The house was boarded up, the side porch was falling off, and the front lawn was growing up in weeds. That hurt much more than hearing it had burned down.

Soon after I got home from Malaysia, my sister and I drove down to Lovejoy to make some cuttings of plants that were special to us. I knew they would soon be killed by scavengers trying to wrestle them out of the ground. As we stepped out of the car, there were ghosts everywhere. Not the ghosts of the slain Confederate soldiers that long ago scared Willie and Ludie as they walked home at night, but the ghosts of parties on the lawn, friends and family coming for syllabub at Christmas, and daffodil picking at Easter. I could almost see Momma in her garden smock with pruners in hand and Dad making camellia grafts on the kitchen counter.

Steering clear of the burned rubble, my sister and I walked to the gardens. The trellises that held the beautiful Sweet Autumn clematis were gone, and with them all the vines. I could tell where my room had been by the big pine tree that stood outside the window by my bed. I remembered my fear when the pungent sabadilla dust floated in my window and I thought for sure that the Germans had arrived.

We walked through what was left of the gardens. I

found several big camellias and took some cuttings, hoping one might be Momma's favorite, a Sawada's Dream which Tom Sawada had sent her many years before. I dug several small sprouts underneath the huge meratia which bloomed every Christmas. Early on Christmas morning, Dad used to bring in a tiny branch with a few open blossoms to add to the holiday decorations over the fireplace. The warm room brought out their fresh sweet fragrance, which greeted my sister and me as we raced down the stairs to search for our presents under the Christmas tree.

I looked up and saw my sweet gum tree standing tall and proud as if it were guarding the ruins. The last time I climbed up into its branches to watch what was going on, I thought it was the biggest and best tree in the world. Almost sixty years later it was a real monster, and still the best-looking tree in back of where the house once stood.

When my sister and I started out the long driveway, I looked back. One of the huge magnolias on the lawn still had a funny-looking top from its encounter with the baseball so many years before. I forgot to look for the chinaberry tree halfway down the drive, since we were old enough to go all the way to the highway by ourselves now. But I could still hear Dad's repeated warning to us children, "Don't go past the chinaberry tree."

Floweracres at Lovejoy wasn't my whole life or even a major part of it. It was the memorable beginning of a life spent growing things in many places around the world. Maybe it's because home is always wonderful when you are small, but my sweet gum tree, the work in the fields, Momma's gardens, and Dad's admonitions remain embedded in my soul and continue to sustain my love of plants.

I thank God every day that from my springtime at Lovejoy and on through my current season at Sweet Apple, my harvest has been so rich.